D0141704

Nineteenth-Century

AMERICAN MUSICAL
THEATER

General Editor
DEANE L. ROOT
University of Pittsburgh

A GARLAND SERIES

Library Property
Do Not Mark In Score

VOLUME 2

Early Melodrama in America

The Voice of Nature *(1803)*

Edited by
Karl Kroeger
University of Colorado

and

The Aethiop *(1813)*

Orchestral Restoration by
Victor Fell Yellin
New York University

GARLAND PUBLISHING, INC.
NEW YORK AND LONDON 1994

The Voice of Nature, Introduction, Incidental music copyright © 1994 by Karl Kroeger
The Aethiop, Introduction, Orchestral score copyright © 1994 by Victor Fell Yellin
All rights reserved

Library of Congress Cataloging-in-Publication Data

Early melodrama in America.
 1 score.—(Nineteenth-century American musical theater; v. 2)
 The 1st play, by William Dunlap, incidental music by Victor Pelissier; the 2nd play, by William Dimond, incidental music by Rayner Taylor.
 The music to the 1st play edited by Karl Kroeger from parts in the New York Public Library; music to the 2nd play reconstructed by Victor Fell Yellin from a contemporary piano score in the Edna Kuhn Loeb Library at Harvard.
 First work previously published: New York: D. Longworth, 1807. 2nd work previously published: The Aethiop, or, The child of the desert. New York: D. Longworth, 1813.
 Includes bibliographical references.
 Contents: The Voice of Nature (1803)—The Aethiop (1813).
ISBN 0-8153-1374-8
1. Incidental music—Scores. I. Kroeger, Karl. II. Yellin, Victor Fell. III. Pelissier, Victor. Voice of nature. 1994. IV. Dunlap, William, 1766–1839. Voice of nature. V. Taylor, R. (Raynor), 1747–1825. Aethiop. 1994. VI. Dimond, William, fl. 1800–1830. Ethiop. 1994. VII. Series.
M1510.E2   1994   93–50849
                                                                       CIP

Book design by Patti Hefner

Printed on acid-free, 250-year-life paper
Manufactured in the United States of America

CONTENTS

INTRODUCTION TO THE SERIES

This series of sixteen volumes provides for the first time ever a comprehensive set of works from a full century of musical theater in the United States of America. Many of the volumes contain musical scores and librettos that have never before been published. Others make available works that were long lost, or widely scattered, or never before assembled in one place. Collectively, this series is the first substantial modern printing, not only of the individual titles it contains, but also of a repertory that is central to the nation's cultural history.

The prevailing view of nineteenth-century American theater is dominated by attention to the *words* voiced by the actors. But for most of this period theater simply did not operate from written texts alone; music was an equal and essential partner with the script. Music was so ubiquitous in the American theater throughout the nineteenth century that any understanding of the subject—or of individual works or theaters, indeed even of specific performances or performers—must take it into account. Yet few scholarly studies and still fewer modern editions of works have included the music as fully as the text. (An excellent summary of recent research, and of the problems created by lack of access to original complete works, is presented in Shapiro, 1987.)

Moreover, this series should help balance an emphasis in the scholarly literature on the bibliography of pre-1800 works at one end and the history and criticism of twentieth-century shows at the other, by providing a substantial body of material in between. Almost without exception, the works published here have been unavailable—even unknown except by reputation—to all but a handful of specialists. As Joseph Kerman has pointed out in his book challenging the field of musicology, research on musical theater is forty years behind most of the western music genres in that its "central texts" (the works themselves) have remained unavailable (Kerman, 1985, p. 48). In a sense, this series is a throwback to an earlier style of anthology delineated by geographical, chronological, and genre bounds, such as helped define historical national repertories for European scholars in the mid-twentieth century.

Until now, only a very few individual nineteenth-century musical-theater works have been issued in modern publications, sometimes—but not always—with the score alongside the libretto. Among the major scholarly series of editions that include musical-theater works performed in nineteenth-century America is A-R Editions' Recent Researches in American Music, which has made available William Shields's *The Poor Soldier* (1783), George F. Root's "operatic cantata" *The Haymakers* (1857), and Victor Pelissier's *Columbian Melodies* (1812) used in New York and Philadelphia theaters. A series from G.K. Hall, titled Three Centuries of American Music, has a single volume devoted to eighteenth- and nineteenth-century *American Opera and Music for the Stage* (1990), containing piano-vocal scores of Alexander Reinagle's *The Volunteers*, Rayner Taylor's *The Ethiop*, Arthur Clifton's *The Enterprise*, and Reginald de Koven's *Robin Hood*. And an English series of Music for London Entertainment 1660–1800, issued by Richard MacNutt (Tunbridge Wells) and later by Stainer & Bell (London), reproduces some works that were also performed in America.

Presented here by Garland Publishing, Inc., with full text and music, the forty-nine works in this series of sixteen volumes are now accessible not only to scholars of music, theater, literature, American studies, and other fields in the humanities and performing arts, but also to teachers and students in the classroom. Every work could be produced again on the stage, either as historic re-creation or in modern adaptation. The purpose of the undertaking is to make full works readily available for analysis, drama criticism, performance, and any other use by a modern academic audience as well as the general public.

The vast majority of surviving sources have lain scattered and hidden in public and private collections throughout the country, awaiting research that would piece them back together. At the time they were part of the living tradition of nineteenth-century American theater, such performance materials were considered functional and ephemeral. Their creators and users had little interest in preserving the works for posterity; they were much more mindful of the production at hand, of the business of attracting an audience and gaining its favor. If that meant keeping all the music scores in a trunk in a theater building prone to fire, or using scripts filled with up-to-the-minute changes, handwritten instructions, and typographical errors, or creating instrumental arrangements and musical insertions to the show without benefit of fully written-out scores, such were the necessities of life. Consequently they kept little, and published even less. (Sometimes their heirs, for whatever family interests they may have had, restricted access to the surviving sources for as much as a century. And even those materials that found their way into accessible archives have not been immune to loss by deterioration, misshelving, and pilferage.)

Most of the music that survives is in piano-vocal reduction from the theater-orchestra arrangements actually used. Much of it was printed and sold as souvenir selections for the musically literate public to use at leisure in their homes. Printed librettos were sold so that the audience could follow the performance at the theater.

This series strikes a balance between the more readily available printed piano-vocal selections and librettos, and the manuscript sources. In some cases, printed or manuscript musical excerpts have been reassembled to re-create a score the public never saw but which comes as close as possible to the melodies and harmonies that the theater musicians performed. In other volumes, the editors have drawn on contemporary sources to re-create the now-lost orchestration of the original theater arrangers (who would normally have been the resident conductors), or to assemble a full score from surviving orchestral parts. In only a few cases, original scores or librettos too indistinct or deteriorated to reproduce have been reset for clarity; we have sought to emphasize the value of seeing (reproducing) the *original* performance materials used in American theaters of the time. In every volume, the conditions of all known original sources and the circumstances surrounding their presentation in this series are clearly identified. Moreover, whenever possible the original sources are reproduced at actual size (although some have been altered slightly to fit the margins of modern printed books). Dates given in volume subtitles indicate the productions of the shows that generated the sources chosen to be reproduced.

The series aims to represent all the major genres and styles of musical theater of the century, from ballad opera through melodrama, plays with incidental music, parlor entertainments, pastiche, temperance shows, ethnic theater, minstrelsy, and operetta, to grand opera. These works reflect vividly the cultural mix of America: the incendiary *Uncle Tom's Cabin* stands alongside later shows written and performed by African-American troupes; the Irish and Yiddish theater in New York used language that modern audiences might not understand, but which was part of everyday life in the ghetto. At one end of the chronological spectrum we have shows imported by British immigrant musicians; at the other stands a grand opera written by the conductor of the Metropolitan Opera House, based on a great American novel.

The series General Editor has eschewed those titles, no matter how important, that are already available in full modern editions. Missing too are works, no matter how fine, of mostly local interest or regional significance. Nor is the series intended to suggest a core repertory, or a pantheon of masterworks. Rather, it is a selection of works by nineteen scholars active in research on a wide range of theatrical styles and cultural issues of the period.

Each volume of the series is complete in itself. Individual editors have each provided an introduction summarizing the careers and works of the composers and librettists. The introduction informs about the work(s) reproduced, giving dates and circumstances of first performances and any early revivals, origins of the plot and its treatment, and a brief critique explaining the historical importance of the work. The editors identify the locations of all significant original sources for each work, and any significant differences among them; they also note any other available performing materials that might be useful for a revival or detailed study (for example, a conducting score, other piano-vocal scores, instrumental parts, librettos, prompt books, stage designs, photographs, manuscript drafts). If the volume reproduces only a piano-reduction score, the editor's introduction identifies (as much as possible) the original instrumentation used in the theater. Recordings of any modern performances are mentioned, and a bibliography provides leads for further inquiry about the works and their creators. When necessary, notations have been made matching the musical selections of the score with their respective locations in the libretto.

Each volume editor has had principal responsibility for identifying the first or most appropriate copy available of the musical score and libretto. In selecting the copies to be reproduced, further preference has gone to those sources that are clean, untorn, and complete, which could be reprinted unedited. As is the nature of rare sources, the best exemplars are not always perfect ones, and we beg your patience with those that are less than ideal.

It is still true, as Anne Dhu Shapiro pointed out in 1987 (p. 570), that "the incomplete state of basic research in the area of musical theater . . . stands as the chief impediment to a better history." This series is offered with the hope and trust that it will foster greater understanding and contribute materially to the wider appreciation of America's heritage and traditions of musical theater.

Deane L. Root
University of Pittsburgh

WORKS CITED

Shapiro, Anne Dhu. Review of Julian Mates, *America's Musical Stage: Two Hundred Years of Musical Theatre*, in the *Journal of the American Musicological Society* XL/3 (Fall 1987): 565–74.

Kerman, Joseph. *Contemplating Music: Challenges to Musicology*. Cambridge, Mass.: Harvard University Press, 1985.

About this Volume

The enterprise of locating and making accessible complete works of American musical theater from throughout the nineteenth century came nearest foundering at the most distant shore of that gulf separating us from the earlier sources. Like the preceding volume in this series, the present volume contains two works; together these volumes comprise nearly all the known full works that survive from before 1815. This second volume represents the earliest works in this series that were preserved entirely in the United States. Even though the two plays have British origins or influences, the scripts used for American productions were issued by American publishers, and the music that accompanied them was written in this country.

The work that leads off this volume, *The Voice of Nature*, is generally considered the first melodrama to be performed in America, and the earliest surviving complete work composed for American professional theater. It is also the first to be written by a playwright born in America. We can see even in this early exemplar the later formulas of the virtuous heroine, villain, protector, and comic servant. Music was not used so extensively as later in the century, but it was given important functions to mark entrances and exits, and underscore pathos and tension, joy and despair. The editor, Karl Kroeger, created the camera-ready score reproduced here with a computer music-processor and a laser printer, setting his reconstruction of the full score from the composer's original manuscript parts held in the Music Division of the New York Public Library at Lincoln Center. During his years as head of the Americana Collection there, he uncovered a number of early works that he has subsequently edited for publication.

Dr. Kroeger, who has his Ph.D. from Brown University (1976) and since 1982 has been Music Librarian and Professor of Music at the University of Colorado at Boulder, is a composer in his own right, and has written extensively about early American music. He edited three volumes of *The Complete Works of William Billings* for the American Musicological Society (Boston, 1977–90), and *Pelissier's Columbian Melodies: Music of the New York and Philadelphia Stages, 1792–1812* (Madison, Wisc.: A-R Editions, 1984).

The work that completes the volume, *The Aethiop; or, The Child of the Desert*, had important political implications in England and the young United States. Rather than reconstructing the composer's original full score (since no orchestral score or parts survive), the editor, Victor Fell Yellin, has re-created an orchestration from the printed pianoforte score. In so doing, he revives an institution long since abandoned, a practice applied to every score imported from abroad before it could be performed in the United States, and to most scores when they were passed (or pirated) from one theater to another. His vivid instrumentation reveals to us how pale the sheet music is as a representation of sound heard in the theater, whether serving contemporary amateur pianists at home, or standing alone as the surviving musical material from shows a century or more after they held the stage.

Dr. Yellin, one of the foremost scholars of early American music, is also the author of *Chadwick, Yankee Composer* (Smithsonian Institution Press, 1990) and *The Operas of Virgil Thomson* (in *Virgil Thomson, American Music Since 1910*, 1970). Excerpts from his opera *ABAYLAR* have been performed by the Metropolitan Opera Studio and Composers Showcase in New York City, where he is Professor of Music at New York University.

D.L.R.

SOURCES

1. *The Voice of Nature* libretto, courtesy of Clements Library, The University of Michigan.

2. *The Voice of Nature* score, courtesy of Karl Kroeger.

3. Portrait of William Dimond, *The Aethiop*, courtesy of the Harvard Theatre Collection, Harvard College Library.

4. *The Aethiop*, 1813 text, courtesy of Fales Collection, Bobst Library, New York University.

5. *The Aethiop* orchestral restoration, courtesy of Victor Fell Yellin, made possible in part by a grant from the National Endowment for the Humanities.

THE VOICE OF NATURE

On the evening of February 4, 1803, the small audience that attended New York's Park Theater probably did not realize that they were witnessing the first local performance of a new species of drama that would soon capture the American stage as it had the playhouses of Europe. This was melodrama, a French creation emphasizing certain popular elements found in sentimental and Gothic plays at the end of the eighteenth century. The theatrical historian, Oral Sumner Coad (1917, p.200), described melodrama's formula as consisting of

> a heroine who is all virtue, a deep-dyed villain, a protector who rescues the lovely victim when her distress is at its height, and generally a humorous servant who also champions the cause of the oppressed.

He also noted that melodrama

> was further distinguished by the use of descriptive music; the entrances, the exits, the pathetic scenes, the tense passages were accompanied by orchestral music in keeping with the character or event. . . . Joy, surprise, suspense, despair, and divers other emotions to the action were represented by the musical score. Still other ear-marks of "melodrame" were dances and pageants, relevantly or irrelevantly introduced; pantomime to assist in presenting the most exciting and breathless episodes; and elaborate stage decorations.

The Voice of Nature is generally considered to be the first melodrama to reach America, but it employs only embryonic elements of the fully developed form. Its strongest feature is undoubtedly its sentimental emotional appeal.

Motherhood, feminine virtue, and justice prevailing in the end were subjects that spoke perhaps more strongly to provincial New York audiences than they did to those in London or Paris. These are the dramatic underpinnings of *The Voice of Nature.*

The music for *The Voice of Nature* represents the earliest extant musical score for a complete dramatic production composed for the American theater. Prior to this, we have only excerpts: individual popular songs, dances, entr'actes, and instrumental pieces, usually arranged for piano and simplified for amateur performance. Here we have the complete musical score, in the composer's own orchestral parts, giving us a good idea not only how the music supported the dramatic action, but also the size, makeup, and performing abilities of the theater orchestra and the thespian singers.

The Voice of Nature is American playwright William Dunlap's translation and adaptation of L. C. Caignez's *Le Jugement de Salomon*, produced in Paris in 1802. Caignez's play, set in Biblical Jerusalem, dramatized the well known story of King Solomon's judgement in the case of two mothers contesting ownership of the same child, as told in I Kings, Chapter 3. The play caught the attention of the British playwright, James Boaden, who adapted it for the London stage in 1802. Perhaps realizing that the play had a more universal appeal than merely a portrayal of a Biblical story, Boaden made some significant changes. Retaining the basic story, he set the scene in Sicily, moved the time closer to his own, and changed the names of the characters to reflect the new place and era. William Dunlap certainly knew Boaden's play, for he retained the title, venue, and characters. However, as Coad points out (1917, p.199), Dunlap's text "shows no indebtedness to the English." Dunlap, a shrewd observer of his countrymen's tastes, probably knew that *The Voice of Nature* would strongly appeal to their sentiments. Rather than simply mount a production of Boaden's play, with its inferior dialogue and, at times, stagnant action, Dunlap chose the most useful elements form both Caignez's and Boaden's versions and fashioned his own drama. Dunlap's play opened to a "miserably thin audience" ("Arouet") and "very indifferent houses" ("Minor Critic"), although the critics praised it rather highly, and following the second performance on Saturday, 5 February, poor attendance forced the manager to close the playhouse for two weeks (Odell, vol. 2, p.172). But it went on to enjoy some popularity in America, being revived at fairly regular intervals over the next twenty years (Odell lists later performances in 1805, 1814, 1815, and 1823).

The plot of the play is fairly simple: at an earlier time, the heroine, Lilla, had had a child out of wedlock by the king's brother. Shortly after its birth, the child was stolen and the dead baby of Alzaira substituted. Lilla recognizes her child through a birthmark, and both women bring their claims to King Alfonso, setting up a reenactment of Solomon's judgement. The villain in the play is not a man, as was often the case in later melodramas, but a woman, Alzaira. Her character was so affecting that the actress who played the part in the first New York performance was overcome by her character's inhumanity. "Arouet" wrote:

> In the close of the play, a circumstance of a singular nature took place. When Mrs. Johnson came to express her contrition to the King for the cruel part she had acted toward *Lilla*, her long-stifled feelings could be repressed no longer; injured nature assumed her sway in her bosom, and she burst into a flood of tears which choked her utterance, and rendered her unable to proceed.

She also delivered an epilogue by way of apology, stating that she could not conceive of a woman and a mother acting in the manner of the character she had portrayed.

The playwright, William Dunlap, one of the Federal era's most versatile talents, was also a noted painter, an ardent historian, a perceptive critic of the arts, and for nine years between 1796 and 1805 the manager of the New York theater (Coad 1930). Born in 1766 in Perth Amboy, New Jersey, son of a merchant and china importer, Dunlap showed an early talent as a painter and portraitist. In 1784 his father sent Dunlap to London for a three-year period of study with the artist Benjamin West. In London young Dunlap developed a passion for the theater. Upon his return to New York, he began to write plays, some of which were applauded sufficiently to encourage him toward a theatrical career. In 1796 he purchased one-quarter interest in the Old American Company, New York's theatrical troupe. By 1798 his two other partners, the actors Lewis Hallam and John Hodgkinson, had withdrawn leaving Dunlap in sole control of the New York theater.

For the next seven years, Dunlap was occupied by almost frantic theatrical activity: hiring actors, mounting plays, arranging advertising, and the thousand-and-one other day-to-day tasks connected with running a theater. Besides mounting his own plays, he busily translated and adapted the works of the major French and German playwrights of the day. His success was various; some seasons were profitable but most were not, and in February 1805, Dunlap was forced into bankruptcy. After a short, unsuccessful attempt at miniature portraiture, Dunlap was back at the theater in the spring of 1806, but this time as a salaried general assistant to the new manager, the actor Thomas Abthorpe Cooper.

Following his final departure from the playhouse in 1811, Dunlap returned to painting, briefly edited a monthly magazine, held a salaried post with the New York state militia, and taught painting at the National Academy of Design, an institution he helped to found. His pen continued its prolific activity, but in fiction, biography, and history, not drama. Beginning in 1813, he published a series of works, the most important of which were his *History of the American Theatre* (1832) and his *History of the Rise and Progress of the Arts of Design in the United States* (1834). Dunlap's death in New York in 1839 brought to an end an astonishingly versatile career. Among the many fields in which he worked, perhaps his most substantial contributions were made as a playwright, where his approximately thirty original plays and a similar number of adaptations earned him the title, "father of American drama" (Coad 1930, p. 518).

Victor Pelissier (ca. 1745–ca.1820) was the principal composer and arranger for the New York theater during Dunlap's management and a French horn player in the theater orchestra (Kroeger 1984). A prolific and versatile composer, Pelissier was a Frenchman who first appeared on the American scene in 1792 as a refugee from the bloody native revolts on the Caribbean island of San Domingue. After about a year in Philadelphia, Pelissier moved to New York in 1793, where he remained until about 1807 working as a theater musician. In 1807 he was engaged by the Philadelphia theater to write music for its plays and to play in its orchestra. Already an elderly man with poor eyesight in 1807, age and blindness forced Pelissier to retire in 1813. He returned to New York where several concerts were held for his benefit in 1814 and 1817, after which he completely faded from view.

During his American careers, Pelissier composed music for at least forty-two plays and arranged and adapted music for an equal number of others. His music, some of which was published in piano arrangements in *Pelissier's Columbian Melodies* in 1812, shows him to have been a talented and experienced musical technician, whose ability to produce a dramatic musical effect was perhaps unsurpassed in America during his day.

The music for *The Voice of Nature* consists of four pieces, scored for a solo soprano, a three-part chorus, and a small orchestra comprising a flute, two oboes, a bassoon, two French horns, and strings. (In the manuscript parts the flute and oboe 1 share the same part, indicating that both instruments were played by the same player.) The four musical numbers are a march, a dance-like Allegro, and two marches with attached choruses, the second of which (No. 4) also includes a vocal solo. Musical cues are provided at several points in the first and third acts permitting one to locate rather precisely the scenes that Pelissier's music was intended to accompany. No. 3 is undoubtedly intended for the final scene of Act I, where the words for the chorus appear in the playscript. Similarly, No. 4 accompanies the opening scene of Act III where the text for the chorus and solo is also to be found. No. 1 was probably used for the entrance of King Alfonso and his troupe toward the end of Act I (p. 14 of the playscript), and No. 2 seems to have been intended to accompany the peasants presenting gifts of fruit and flowers to the king (playscript, p. 15 and 16). At the end of Act I, the curtain may have fallen to a repeat of the march in No. 3. The only other musical cues in the play are trumpet fanfares in the first and third acts. These were probably improvised by one of the musicians as needed, for no fanfares are written into Pelissier's score.

Other places where music might have been used in the play are before the acts. The opening march also might have served as a prelude. The march in No. 3 might have introduced Act II and the march in No. 4 also may have prefaced Act III. However, since the orchestra customarily played between acts, both to entertain the audience and cover the noise of the set changes, music unrelated to Pelissier's score may well have introduced each act. Other scenes in the play where music seems to be called for, such as at the end of Act II where Lilla, having discovered her child, looks longingly after him as he is led away, apparently went unscored. In his review, "Arouet" speaks highly of Mrs. Hodgkinson's song in Act I, but no song for the first act appears in Pelissier's score. It was a common practice to add songs and dances to plays for greater audience entertainment. There is no way to tell what Mrs. Hodgkinson may have sung.

The second edition of the playscript for *The Voice of Nature* was used for this edition. It differs little from the first edition, published in 1803, but does correct some typographical errors. The musical score has been constructed from the manuscript vocal and instrumental parts in Pelissier's hand found in the Music Division of the New York Public Library. The parts appear to have been prepared with some care by Pelissier himself, so few editorial changes have been necessary in order to make the music ready for performance. Occasional dynamic markings, articulation marks, and slurs that appear to be missing have been tacitly supplied. Pelissier sometimes marked articulation only at the first measure of several containing the same figuration. It has been assumed that the same signs would have been employed in the succeeding measures by the players. Similarly, repeated passages that appear later in the music either lack or occasionally supply editorial detail. These have been made to agree with one another. Pelissier sometimes added a dynamic mark in one part but omitted it in another. In general, it has been assumed that the same dynamic level prevailed throughout the ensemble, and dynamics have been supplied editorially without comment where they appear to have been omitted.

I wish to thank the New York Public Library for permitting the publication of Pelissier's music, William Kearns for his advice, and Deane Root, the editor of this series, for his help and encouragement.

WORKS CITED

"Arouet." Critic in New York *Evening Post* (February 5, 1803).
Coad, Orville Sumner. *William Dunlap*. New York: The Dunlap Society, 1917.

_____. Biographical sketch of William Dunlap, in *Dictionary of American Biography*, vol. 5, pp. 516–18. New York: C. Scribner's Sons, 1930.

Kroeger, Karl. "Introduction." *Pelissier's Columbian Melodies*. Madison, Wisc.: A-R Editions, 1984. Contains the most complete information on Pelissier's American career.

"Minor Critic." In New York *Morning Chronicle* (February 7, 1803).

Odell, George C. D. *Annals of the New York Stage*, vol. 2. New York: Columbia University Press, 1927.

K.K.

THE AETHIOP; OR, THE CHILD OF THE DESERT

Four months after the beginning of the War of 1812, when the fledgling United States declared its independence from Britain a second time in a generation, a "New Grand Romantick Drama" called *The Aethiop; or, The Child of the Desert* by William Dimond was given in a most lavish manner on 13 October at Covent Garden, London, with music by Henry Rowley Bishop. It was a fiasco. But, despite war and failure, *The Aethiop* made its way across the sea. In April 1813, with new music (now lost) by James Perossier, the show had a limited run in New York City, even while American defeats on land were creating a gloomy mood, such was the great demand for stage entertainment. The British musical was again taken up, this time for the fall season at the Chestnut Street Theatre, Philadelphia. There, a unique production was offered to the public "in a style of splendour never exceeded on the American stage . . . with entire new scenery, dresses, and decorations." "Mr. R. Taylor" was billed as composer of original "music and accompaniments," and piano scores were advertised for sale at the box office, so sanguine were expectations of success. Substitution of patriotic spectacles celebrating the much-hoped-for American naval victories, however, postponed the premiere of *The Aethiop* until New Year's Day, 1814.

This brief account not only proves the intimate connection between the London and American stages, even during a fratricidal conflict, it also is instructive of the way complicated and stylish London novelties were realized here. Especially in the case of the innovative genre I have elsewhere labelled "London Melodrama," where conventional distinctions between the spoken drama and opera are deliberately blurred, only the text was usually published. A success might spur the printing of a keyboard souvenir intended for home performance. But the orchestral score remained the property of the theater company. Thus, even when a souvenir keyboard score existed, it was still necessary for any other production to hire someone to re-create an orchestral version. Indeed, an important occupation for many Eastern seaboard musicians was the fabrication of instrumental "accompaniments," based upon published souvenir scores, for American productions of London musicals.

In the case of *The Aethiop*, its London failure precluded any keyboard score publication of Bishop's music. It was necessary to commission entirely new music for both the New York and Philadelphia productions, and it was to this special circumstance that we owe Rayner Taylor's exceptional score. Interestingly enough, when a Boston *Aethiop* (25 March 1815) was contemplated little over a year later, at a time when Taylor's complete orchestral score and parts existed in Philadelphia, John Bray, the sometime singing comedian and composer of *The Indian Princess* (Philadelphia, 1808), then resident in Boston, was, nevertheless, hired to make a new orchestral score from Taylor's published pianoforte music.

What, then, happened to Taylor's own orchestral score and its instrumental parts, the property of the Chestnut Street Theatre? The sad answer to this question is that these materials were, in all likelihood, destroyed along with the theater in an 1820 conflagration. That Taylor's music survived at all is due to George E. Blake's print of the pianoforte score. It also may very well be that the copy upon which the present orchestral restoration is based—now preserved at the Eda Kuhn Loeb Library at Harvard—was the one employed by Bray for his arrangement of his colleague's music.

Taylor's *Aethiop* music may be considered American because it was composed and performed in Philadelphia during the Federal period. Nevertheless, this fact should not obscure its essentially English style or, indeed, the English nature of the American stage at the time. Born in London, Taylor (1747–1825) was a boy in the Chapel Royal, organist at Chelmsford, and music director at Sadler's Wells when, near the age of fifty, he suddenly departed London in the company of an ingenue for an uncertain future in America. William Dimond (1783–1837), the playwright, was the namesake son of a most well-known collaborator of the illustrious English actor, David Garrick. In fact, almost all the members of the Philadelphia theater were British by birth. Doubtless one reason why the company delayed the opening of *The Aethiop* to present tableaux in honor of American naval heroes in the battles against England was to allay any suspicion of secret allegiance to their former homeland.

Both the main and subplot of *The Aethiop* exhibit the concerns of fashionable, early nineteenth-century theatergoers with exotica, especially of the Near East, fueled by romantic translations of the *Thousand and One Night's Tales* and Napoleon's 1798 expedition to Egypt. The glorification of an Arab ruler in the drama also demonstrates the great change in the xenophobic feelings of Christendom towards Islam that occurred during the period.

Fabled Haroun Al-Raschid of Baghdad is the noble, all-wise hero of the story who, by assuming the disguise of a Black necromancer (the Aethiop), is able to infiltrate the band of a rebellious pretender to this throne. He gains their confidence, and, ultimately, reconciles their differences with him without bloodshed. To London society during the Regency, Dimond pleads tolerance by combining positive qualities of Muslims and Blacks in one heroic character and makes a gesture for orderly dynastic succession at a time when George III, declared insane, was succeeded by his dissolute son. This serious plot is balanced by a domestic comedy. To the gallery, Dimond appeals to popular prejudice. The comic subplot deals chauvinistically with the vicissitudes of a young Greek Christian couple trying to eke out an existence in Baghdad by selling contraband liquor. The lecherous advances to the beautiful wife, Zoe, by two venal Arab officials are thwarted when, informed of their intentions, their wives appear.

Why such a seemingly innocuous pair of tales should have raised the ire of conservative London critics is difficult to understand today. Similar plots have long since become dramatic clichés. In the context of the times, however, some could well object to the presence of "diabolism" indicated by the Aethiop's "magic" wand. Still others might carp at the apparent condonation of marital infidelity implied by Zoe's willingness to make assignations. Perhaps every bit as objectionable was the novel genre of London melodrama in which all the theatrical arts were given equal standing to the disadvantage of poetry, an innovation seen by many litterateurs as a threat to culture and a blatant appeal to the uneducated. Finally, and even more damaging to the success of *The Aethiop*, were the *ad hominem* attacks on the melodramatists themselves for their flamboyant behavior, their dandyism, and their homosexuality. Dimond eventually was forced, under threat of prison, to flee to the Continent.

In Philadelphia, far from the tangled politics and personalities of London, such intrigues were absent. Judged on its merit as theater alone, *The Aethiop* was the biggest box-office and critical success up to that time and for many years to come. It had record receipts of $1,607.25 for its first performance. From Boston to New Orleans, *The Aethiop* held the stage until the Civil War. It is paradoxical that so complex a work, anticipating many now-established elements of modern dramaturgy, should have failed in cosmopolitan London and succeeded in the naive City of Brotherly Love.

The architecture of *The Aethiop* is on a grand scale. Combination of a dynastic thriller with a domestic comedy requires a rapid sequential order to create the illusion of simultaneous action so dear to today's cinemasters. Double-plotting also demands double-casting. Here is where the simple lines of conventional drama cross. The main plot is projected by actors in the Shakespearian tradition who declaim words in blank verse. Music required for these scenes, restricted to the ceremonial, is mainly orchestral and choral. Personal sentiments, expressed in rolling elocution rather than in melody, are sometimes accompanied by instruments. In only one instance is a truly operatic device—accompanied recitative—employed. Occasions for independent instrumental dances are provided to show the luxury and opulence of the Saracen court and, no doubt, to display the charms of the feminine form. But nowhere in the high drama is there room for the aria.

Unlike the main plot, the secondary story is told as a comic opera where the protagonists emote in song connected by colloquial dialogue. Only one number of the subplot is conceived in a more complex, narrative format.

For both plots, Taylor writes a musical score of flexibility and evocation. In his sixty-sixth year, having largely abjured the career of theatrical composer, the Nestor of American musicians seems to have taken on the Chestnut Street commission with relish. He apparently did not feel constrained to condescend, as one might have expected given the provincial setting, to an unsophisticated audience, nor did he have to make allowances for inferior musical forces. Clearly, Taylor's score is itself proof of the elevated taste of Philadelphia. Relying on the combined background of church musician and theater composer, he constructed an extraordinary work. Comparison with the music of the much younger Bishop, twenty-six at the time of the Covent Garden flop, is very favorable to the more ancient composer. One might even venture to say that an important reason for *The Aethiop*'s success in Philadelphia was its Taylor music.

Following the scenario of Dimond's drama, the music for *The Aethiop* as conceived by Taylor is episodic and written in separate numbers, or counts cued to specific indications in the dialogue. The listener may discern various genres and types of baroque-classical style. Yet, there is a certain consistency of manner unified by common-practice harmony and idiomatic melody. For example, music descriptive of the pomp and ceremony of Al-Raschid's court recalls Handelian sonorities. More spirited scenes devoted to the machinations of the conspirators have a late-eighteenth-century flavor created by imaginative use of natural brass and percussion energized by busy swooping scale passages. Here and there, as in the chorus "Child of the Desert Awful Rise," we hear striking chromatic harmonies. The overture provides another musical blend of the three main affects of the drama: mystery, comedy, and nobility in a Haydn manner. After a slow introduction, a fast rondo form—with variations for key performers—ends with a stirring finale where the comedic woodwind tune is ennobled by assignment to the unison orchestra.

For the comic subplot, Taylor's experience as a performer and music director-composer for various London pleasure gardens stood him in good stead in composing a sequence of delightful pieces. Though the songs are nothing more than strophic ditties, they all seem to have an up-to-date—even Mozartian—flavor, doubtless a tribute to the Austrian master's influence through his English disciples, the siblings Stephen and Nancy Storace, Michael Kelly, and Thomas Attwood.

"The Musical Colloquy," in particular, is noteworthy for the way in which Taylor adapts a more complex operatic form to the simpler needs of London melodrama. Designed by Dimond as a tiny finale, the action in the Bezestein or marketplace is meant to be wholly set to music. Benmoussaff, the cadi, humiliated by the young Greek couple, Alexis and Zoe, revenges himself by having Alexis arrested for selling liquor in repudiation of their bargain. Alexis protests this betrayal as guards lead him off to prison. Zoe pleads for her husband's release. Alexis bemoans his fate, but to no avail as he is dragged away to the accompaniment of the hostile crowd's shouts. Although the entire scene takes but a minute and a half, the "Musical Colloquy" effectively stages, by means of music, the varying emotions and actions of the three main comedic characters,

Turkish Guards, and the assorted denizens of the Baghdad bazaar.

If the historical precedent for orchestral restoration of theatrical keyboard souvenir scores is quite clear, the nature and extent of the process is not. To date, neither have such restorations come to light, nor are there, apparently, handbooks describing the practice. Also, the surviving piano scores, intended for amateurs, lack detail. Thus, many questions of an artistic and philosophical nature arise. How much musical flesh and cosmetic may be applied to the bare bones? Like the anthropological sculptor preparing figures for museum display, the orchestral restorer must choose among different blends of authenticity and imagination.

Taylor's keyboard score, then, is concerned mainly with stimulating recollection of the actual theatrical experience of the music rather than with representation of his complete artistic conception or even with providing a blueprint for piratical production. It is merely a simplified version of the orchestral music, a skeletal arrangement on only two staves: the treble devoted to the tunes underlaid with text; the bass assigned the accompaniment, with nothing in between.

Despite this lack of complete information, many numbers are not difficult to reconstruct orchestrally. For example, Taylor implies the orchestration of the "Overture" by using such terms as *Unis.* (for "unison," or the whole orchestra), *Clarinetto, Flauto, tutti, piz* (for "pizzicato"), *Solo Violin*, and *Solo Violincello* [sic]. In other places, orchestral figurations typical of string accompaniments are indicated in miniscule noteheads attached to the notes of the vocal line, as in "Corner Houses," or at cadential endings when the treble staff is not occupied by the tune and text, as in "These Keys Can a Treasure Unfold." "The Turkish Guards March," where the scenario as well as the melodic and harmonic structure betoken the sonorities of brass, percussion, and "Turkish" instruments, is another example of a piece whose orchestration seems to be predetermined by its genre.

The most challenging task of restoration was the "Musical Colloquy." Except for the initial C major chords in five parts, indications of the harmony for chorus, and a cadential string figuration, there are no usable clues to the Philadelphia composer's orchestral intentions. As the piano music stands, only the melody accompanied by a single bass line is presented. For those who heard the actual theater performance, such a skeleton score would have been sufficient to evoke the original sonorities. The notes alone on the souvenir score provide but a mere shadow of the musical reality. In my attempt to recreate the orchestral sounds of the "Colloquy" I seized upon the three measures of string-like figurations at the first major cadence to invent a countermelody conceived in similar running sixteenth notes. This orchestral figure, supported by the original bass line and complemented by my string syncopations and wind punctuations, provides an atmosphere of agitation demanded by the action. Also, by its varied repetition the new obbligato gives cohesion and shape to the narrative structure of the scene. In so doing I have assumed that a composer of Taylor's experience and imagination would have employed his orchestra similarly.

Orchestral restoration of such a skeleton score must also take into account the nature and size of the musical forces involved in the production. The singers and orchestra of the Chestnut Street Theatre always had had the reputation of being the best in America, due to the predilections of its founding co-manager, Taylor's erstwhile student, Alexander Reinagle (1756–1809), himself a professional musician and composer of merit. But the sumptuousness of the musical forces assembled to perform *The Aethiop* was not universally hailed. William B. Wood, actor-manager of the Chestnut Street Theatre at the time, who had the double responsibility of playing the part of Almanzor, chief villain of the piece, and running the company, complained that, in spite of the success of a musical melodrama—two to three times the usual revenue—actual profit was reduced by the costs incurred. According to Wood, "the extra expenditure for a larger chorus force, additional performers . . . added to the enormous demands of the principal singers" had to be factored in. The salaried orchestra often had to be augmented by casual instrumentalists paid by the performance and by gentlemen amateurs or students eager to participate for free tickets. Wood's testimony would seem to confirm the view that Taylor was writing for a large musical ensemble. No doubt, these circumstances, decried by the theater director, may very well have been one of the main attractions for Taylor, the superannuated composer who must have seen in the commission a chance for one last hurrah.

The modern restorer also has to pay attention to the idiosyncratic techniques and sounds of preindustrial musical instruments. Particularly in the case of natural brass, i.e., trumpets and horns without pistons or valves, care must be taken in chromatic or tonally unstable passages. Such instruments are generally limited to the diatonic tones of the harmonic series. However, a passage like the terminal codetta of "The Subterranean Chorus" seems to demand eerie sonorities that may be supplied only by chromatic modification of the natural horn tones: "a thin quivering flame now springs up, and flickers about the edge of the chasm—Almanzor, and the Aethiop each seize upon a hand of the kneeling boy, and forcibly lead him to the brink of the chasm." Exceptional though they may be, artificial chromatics on the horn were used to create such atmospheres of suspense and mystery during the period and it would seem logical to assume that Taylor intended a similar orchestral sound.

A word about the format of the present orchestral score: In order to avoid the often tedious apparatus of a *Revisionsbericht* or list of differences between the original and orchestrally restored versions of *The Aethiop* music, and to provide a piano accompaniment, the Philadelphia print of Taylor's souvenir is here faithfully copied, measure for measure, underneath the modern orchestral score. The interested reader may thus easily compare one with the other to make instantaneous judgments as to the authenticity or propriety of the restoration. Such a juxtaposition also makes it possible, immediately, to discern correction of obvious errors in the original print, including misprints, missing or dropped measures, and unintentionally awkward passages. Likewise, all editorial additions in the orchestral score, dynamic indications, phrasing and bowing marks, and measure numbers may be collated with the source at a glance.

Except for the three exemplars of Blake's Philadelphia publication of 1813, Taylor's music for *The Aethiop* has vanished. The complete and almost pristine copy used for the present restoration is at Harvard. A defective copy is in the collection of the Library of Congress, and a third deeply foxed and water-stained copy was recently located in the library of the Moravian Music Foundation at Winston-Salem, North Carolina. George E. Blake (1775–1871), the long-lived music publisher, was an active musical amateur as well as sage businessman. His Philadelphia shop was next to the studio and residence of the celebrated portraitist, Thomas Sully (1783–1872), where both men, together with Taylor and other members of the Musical Fund Society, met and gave recitals. Blake's edition of *The Aethiop* (or *Ethiop*, as he spelled it on the title page) was one of his most elaborate issues. For it he commissioned an engraving by the young artist and future architect of the United States Treasury in Philadelphia, William Strickland (1787–1854), who chose as his subject the moment when Haroun, disguised as the Aethiop, suddenly appears to the conspirators during a lightning storm. Strickland's illustration, a gem in itself, is a token of Philadelphia's interlocking artistic friendships. Besides the engraved title page, sequential numbering of the pages indicates that Blake planned to sell the entire music as a single unit. But he also took the added step of providing fancy headings for almost all of the individual numbers so that they might be sold separately. As mentioned above, the music is printed on systems of only two staves—treble and bass. Such a disposition reduced the considerable cost of engraving by about one third and made the music easier to play, especially for self-accompaniment. Staves were scribed, notes were punched, and the text underlaid, all manually.

The significance of Taylor's music for *The Aethiop* to the cultural history of the United States is as great as it is varied. For one thing, it is further evidence of the sophisticated taste of Philadelphia. Moreover, as one of the few extant scores of dramatic music from the Federal period, it is a rare and charming example of an American composer's craft and imagination. Finally, that such a complex theatrical project as a London melodrama could be mounted with success in America during the midst of war is testimony to the strong artistic ties with England.

Bibliographical Notes

For details, documentation, and other references to facts stated in this introduction, the reader may consult the author's articles in *American Music*. Rayner Taylor's career in England and the United States is covered in "Rayner Taylor," *American Music* 1 (Fall 1983): 48–71. *The Aethiop* itself is discussed in two subsequent articles: "Rayner Taylor's Music for *The Aethiop*: Part 1, Performance History," *American Music* 4 (Fall 1986): 249–67; and "Rayner Taylor's Music for *The Aethiop*: Part 2, The Keyboard Score (*The Ethiop*) and Its Orchestral Restoration," *American Music* 5 (Spring 1987): 20–47. These two articles give specific bibliographical, biographical, historical, and analytical information as well as selected musical examples.

Those contemplating theatrical production of *The Aethiop* may also consult Susan L. Porter's *With an Air Debonair: Musical Theatre in America, 1785–1815* (Washington, D.C.: Smithsonian Institution Press, 1991), for practical discussions of stage matters and performance practice during the Federal period. Allardyce Nicoll's *A History of Early Nineteenth Century Drama* in his six-volume *A History of English Drama 1660–1900* (Cambridge: Cambridge University Press, 1952–59), the standard history, gives interesting details of the innovative dramaturgy of London melodrama. Another informative, and sympathetic, view of the performance traditions of the period on both sides of the Atlantic is Joseph Donohue, *Theatre in the Age of Kean* (Oxford: Basil Blackwell, 1975).

A recording of the Taylor-Yellin orchestral score of music for *The Aethiop*, performed on original instruments (such as natural brass) by the the orchestra, chorus, and soloists of The Federal Music Society, is available on New World Records NWR 232. For a review, see Peter G. Davis, "A Landmark Series of American Music Recordings," in *The New York Times* (January 14, 1976).

The print of the music for *The Aethiop* (spelled *Ethiop*) upon which this orchestral restoration is based was published by George E. Blake in Philadelphia in 1813, a date confirmed by advertisements in *Poulson's American Daily Advertiser* in December of that year. Besides the variant spelling of *Aethiop*, doubtless due to the influence of Noah Webster's reforms, the title page misspells the name of the author of the play, William Dimond as "Diamond." Further orthographic variants between the Blake print of Taylor's music and the text of the drama are "Caphania" for "Cephania," and "Arasmin" for "Orasmyn." Other anomalies between the keyboard score and the play text are the omission in Taylor's music of Constantine's air "My dark-eyed maid" and the septetto "La lira! La lira!" (which in effect is the last number of the comic subplot). Measuring approximately 9 by 12 $\frac{1}{2}$ inches, the copper-plate engravings (actually scribed staves and punched notation) number twenty-five pages. For information on Blake see Donald William Krummel, "Philadelphia Music Engraving and Publishing, 1800–1890" (Ph.D. dissertation, University of Michigan, 1958).

V.F.Y.

INDEX OF MUSICAL NUMBERS

THE VOICE OF NATURE

THE AETHIOP

THE VOICE OF NATURE

District of } *ss.* B E IT REMEMBERED, that in
New-York. } the thirty-first year of the Independence of the United
States of America, *David Longworth*, of the said District, hath deposited in this office, the title of a Book,
the right whereof he claims as proprietor, in the words
and figures following, to wit :

" *The Voice of Nature : a drama, in three acts. Translated and altered from a french Melo-drame, called
the Judgment of Solomon By William Dunlap, esq.
As performed at the New-York Theatre. From the
prompt book.*"

In conformity to the Act of the Congress of the United
States, entitled " An Act for the encouragement of
" Learning, by securing the Copies of Maps, Charts,
" and Books, to the Authors and Proprietors of such
" Copies, during the times herein mentioned ;" and al-
" so to an act entitled " An Act supplementary to an
" act entitled, An Act for the encouragement of Learn-
" ing by securing the copies of Maps, Charts, and
" Books, to the Authors and Proprietors of such Copies,
" during the times therein mentioned, and extending
" the benefits thereof, to the Arts of Designing, Engrav-
" ing and Etching historical and other prints."
EDWARD DUNSCOMB,
Clerk of the District of New-York.

THE

VOICE OF NATURE:

A DRAMA,

IN THREE ACTS.

Translated and altered from a french Melo-drame, called

THE JUDGMENT OF SOLOMON.

BY WILLIAM DUNLAP, ESQ.

As performed at the New-York Theatre.

FROM THE PROMPT-BOOK.

SECOND EDITION.

THE PROPERTY OF THE LONG ISLAND HIST

NEW-YORK:

PUBLISHED BY DAVID LONGWORTH,
At the Dramatic Repository,
Shakspeare Gallery.
1807.

DRAMATIS PERSONÆ.

Alphonso, *king of Sicily* .	Mr. FENNEL.
Rinaldo, *his brother* .	Mr. HODGKINSON.
Pedro	Mr. HALLAM, jun.
Vasquez	Mr. JOHNSON.
Child	Miss HODGKINSON.
Clarinda . , . .	Mrs. JEFFERSON.
Alzaira	Mrs. JOHNSON.
Benedetta . . .	Mrs. HOGG.
Lilla	Mrs. HODKINSON.
Isabella . . .	Miss BRETT.

Laborers, peasants, courtiers, soldiers, &c.

. . . .

SCENE—SICILY.

4

VOICE OF NATURE.

ACT I.

SCENE—*a garden. An arbor which laborers are decorating with garlands, is somewhat back.*

enter VASQUEZ, *followed by* BENDETTA *and* LILLA.

Vasq. Come in, come in—here you will see all the show : the king that *is*, and the queen that *is to be ;* and the brave prince Rinaldo, who has been all the way to Naples, to bring his brother a wife—and the lords and the ladies—and here you will not be crowded and squeezed as the people are outside the gates—make yourselves comfortable. (*goes towards the bower*)

Bend. Thank you, cousin, thank you, we'll be quite at home. Lord, lord ! what it is to have a friend at court. Could any thing be more lucky than to find my cousin Vasquez here, head gardener at the king's country palace of Oretto. I always said Vasquez was a good fellow, he dont desert his friends because he's become a great man.

Vasq. (to laborers) Very well. That will do. Now go finish the bowers on the bank of the river. Bustle—the king will soon be here. (*comes forward and speaks to* Bendetta) The lady Clarinda, our future queen is not far off—several couriers have passed on to Palermo—and the king is already

A 2

on his way from the city, hither to meet his bride. To-morrow will be the day !—if you have a mind to go to Palermo to-morrow, you will see such a wedding and such doings as never were seen in Sicily before.

Lilla Is it *certain*, sir, that prince Rinaldo, the king's brother, who went to Naples for the lady, will return with her ?

Vasq. Yes, my pretty maid.

Lilla. (*aside*) Then I shall see him again (*to* Vasquez) And you think, sir, that the lady Clarinda will stop here as she passes ?

Vasq. To be sure she will if its only to see my gardens. Why all these preparations are on her account. Besides, this palace is right in her way. From the upper part of the garden, you may see the road she must come. (Lilla *goes up and occasionally disappears*) Well, my good old cousin, I am very glad to see you again; the sight of you makes me think of good old times.

Bend. Ah, those times are past.

Vasq. To besure they are, but the remembrance is present : and when an honest man calls up the remembrance of past deeds, his conscience smiles, his heart laughs, and the days of his youthful joys are doubled and trebled upon him. But who is that pretty girl ?

Bend. O, the dear soul ! that's my Lilla—o, Vasquez, Vasquez, if ever there was an angel upon earth she's one.

Vasq. Your daughter ?

Bend. No, no. Poor child ! I was her nurse when she was a little, little thing, and now we live together on the banks of the Bagaria, by the work of our hands :—yet Vasquez she was born to rank and fortune ; but all swept away, parents and all, in the cruel wars ! I took her to my cottage a helpless little infant, and unfortunately, poor thing ! she grew up the loveliest girl in the province of Bagaria.

Vasq. Unfortunately !

Bend. Ah, Vasquez ! a young innocent girl, who has the freshness and delicacy of the rose, often experiences the fate of the tender flower she resembles : gently the wind tempts it to expand, then rudely passes over it, and its freshness is withered forever. It is now four years, since a fine handsome young gentleman resided in our neighborhood ; he saw Lilla, and—

Vasq. The wind blew, and the rose withered !

Bend. Alas, poor thing ! innocent and unsuspecting, she believed his promises of marriage—but the rank of the young man destroyed all hopes, for he was not only noble but royal, poor Lilla—

Vasq. What the seducer of your Lilla is—

Bend. Rinaldo.

Vasq. The king's brother !

Bend. The same. We have not seen him since, and Lilla has rejected all letters and presents. But what totally overwhelmed the happiness of my poor girl, was the loss of her child, the very day after its birth ; a healthful, lovely infant !

Vasq. And died so soon !

Bend. No : it still lives for any thing we know. It was carried away while we slept ; and the same perfidious hand left in its stead another new-born infant, but lifeless. To strangers who scarcely look at children so very young, the lifeless boy appeared the child of Lilla—to obtain justice was hopeless, and she wept in silence and in secret. It is three years since this event, and still Lilla weeps for her

boy. She never meets a child of the age her's
would have been, without kissing it and seeking in
its face for the resemblance of her lost infant.

Vasq. Prince Rinaldo! so, so, I see you did not
come from the banks of the Bagaria, only to see the
king's wedding.

Bend. No, Vasquez, my poor Lilla—

Vasq. Does Lilla know, that there is here another
female, who expects the arrival of the prince with
no little impatience?

Bend. Another?

Vasq Yes, another, and more happy than your
poor Lilla, for she is to be married to him.

Bend. Who?

Vasq, The noble lady Alzaira, widow of the lord
Bertoldo.

Bend. I have often heard of her, though to tell
you the truth I never heard much good of her. She
lived in the province of Bagaria in her late husband's time. Is she then here?

Vasq. She arrived yesterday.

Bend. His marriage will not surprise Lilla; a
rumor of the kind had reached us. Poor Lilla,
alas! can have no hope!

Lilla. (*pointing off*) Bendetta! dear Bendetta!
come hither! see yon lovely child coming down
the alley of roses—(Bendetta *goes to her*) see how
he sports among the flowers—not half so fresh as
his cheeks!

Bend. Sweet boy!—Vasquez, whose is that pretty child?

Vasq. That is the son of the late lord Bertoldo
and the lady Alzaira of whom we were speaking.

Lilla. Alzaira!—did you say Alzaira? is it not
said that she is to be married to——

Bend. (*interrupting her*) There is such a report, a mere rumor, but—

Lilla. (*to* Vasquez) Is she handsome?

Vasq. Yes. She has a fine figure and a noble air—but haughty—she is thought handsome—but, as for me, " handsome is that handsome does."

Lilla. Doubtless the prince loves her?

Vasq. That is more than I can tell. When great folks marry we never think of asking that question.

Lilla. (*looking out*) See! see him Bendetta? who is the woman that is with him?

Vasq. Signora Isabella, his governess.

enter ISABELLA *following the child who has something hid in a fold of his sash.*

Lilla. (*approaching the child*) See! what a charming boy, Bendetta! (*to* Isabella) signora, he is a lovely child!

Isab. We all love him, but *too much*—except—(*checks herself.*)

Lilla. Except? *who* but *must* love him!

Bend. Vasquez, dont you think they look alike?

Vasq. They are both pretty—that's all the resemblance I can see.

Lilla. (*to the child*) Will you kiss me? (*the child presents his mouth, she kisses him*) sweet rogue! what are you hiding there? (*the child shows a bird's nest*) good heavens! poor little birds, you have taken them away from their mother! o, the poor mother, when she finds that they are gone? you know not, little angel, you know not, that a mother when she has lost her children weeps for them all her days. (*she wipes her eyes, the child looks at her, then runs off.*)

Isab. He has gone to replace the nest.

Lilla. Look, look.

Bend. He is lost among the bushes.

Lilla. Alas! he would have been of the same age. O, what a consolation had he been to me! yes, the heart that is warmed with maternal fondness would but partialiy feel the pangs of love? o, Bendetta, who knows what would be the effect, if I could this moment place myself before his father, holding by the hand————perhaps I flatter myself; but would not the woman who could place such a child in his arms, have some charms in his eyes?

Bend. Come, come Lilla, think no more on that.

(*the* CHILD *re-enters without the bird's-nest.*)

Child. There!—the mother wont cry any more!

Lilla. (*kissing him*) For the mother I thank you. How happy ought your mother to be!

Vasq. There are more reasons than one that ought to make her love that child—for if it had not been for him—no matter—but signora Isabella knows as well as I.

Lilla. What do you mean, sir?

Isab. I know the common report on the subject, that's all.

Vasq. Who ever doubted the truth of the report?

Lilla. What report?

Isab. Why, in a few words, it is said, that the lord Bertoldo was upon the point of procuring a divorce from Alzaira; and that nothing but the birth and fair promise of this child, prevented him from degrading the lady to her original state, which was not of the first rank.

Bend. Why then if Alzaira does not love a child whose birth was of such consequence to her—

Vasq. And yet that *is* the case.

Lilla. How!!

Isab. Vasquez—

Vasq. Why should I hide my thoughts? though I so seldem see the lady, I have perceived it.

Lilla. What! a mother not love her child! that is impossible! (*the child holds out his arms to* Lilla *who does not see it.*)

Bend. See, he holds out his arms to you.

Lilla. Come to my heart! (*embracing him*)

Child. I love you.

Lilla. You love me! ah, I love you too, sweet boy!

Vasq. (*to* Isabella) Did you ever see his mother kiss him thus?

Isab. Hush! she comes.

enter ALZAIRA *and two ladies as attendants.*

Alz. (*coming forward in the centre*) Vasquez, the king is at hand. Have you fulfilled my orders? is all ready?

Vasq. All my lady.

Alz. Who are these women?

Vasq. A cousin of mine, madam, and her daughter, who have come from Bagaria to be present at the approaching festival.

Lilla. Permit me, madam, to congratulate you, on the happiness of having so lovely a child: I, myself have been a mother, and can therefore readily conceive how exquisite your feelings must be in contemplating this boy. If the infant heaven had given me, had not been stolen from me—

Alz. (surprised and agitated) Stolen ?—a child ?—
Bend. Yes, madam, they stole him from us.
Alz. Who ?
Bend. We know not.
Alz. (takes hold of the child and passes him to her right side) Astonishing ! and you came from Bagaria ?
Lilla. From the banks of the river Bagaria.
                                        (*trumpets*)
Alz. The king ! I go to meet him.   Follow me, Isabella. (*as she is going, she stops, casts a troubled look on* Lilla.   *The child kisses his hand to* Lilla.   *Alzaira sees it and makes the child pass on before her*)
          [*exeunt* Alzaira, child, Isabella *and ladies*
Bend. I do not like her looks.
Lilla. Her countenance makes me tremble.
Vasq. Let us retire.   The king is coming.
                                        (*trumpets*)

enter ALPHONSO *and* ALZAIRA, ISABELLA *and* CHILD, *ladies, officers and guards.*

Alph. Thanks Alzaira, again and again thanks for having undertaken the task of decorating this spot as a resting-place for my queen.   She shall confess that her Italy can not produce more of tasteful beauty than now adorns the banks of the limpid Oretto.
Alz. If my exertions have pleased your majesty—
Alph. They have—and Rinaldo shall thank you. Yes, Alzaira, the interest you have taken in these preparations must be placed to his account as much as mine.

Alz. I hope that your majesty is convinced—

Alph. That you ought to be pleased with my brother's return and the approach of your nuptials. And you, pretty boy, will find in Rinaldo, the father you had lost. I know he loves you—sweet fellow! who does not? *(kisses him)*

enter PEDRO.

Pedro. Sire, we can perceive the approach of the prince and your royal consort.

Alph. Thanks, faithful Pedro, for the joyful tidings. Come lady, let us on and meet them.

[*exeunt* Alphonso, Alzaira, &c. &c.

Lilla. Ah, Bendetta! I feel that I shall lack support.

Bend. Courage, courage! you will soon see him.

enter VASQUEZ.

Vasq. Well, cousin, did you see the king?

Bend. As plain as I see you. O, Vasquez, I could have kissed him when he took the child in his arms. O, it does one good to see that a great man, before whom every body stands in awe, has got a *heart* like common folks.

Vasq. Yes, Bendetta, but Alphonso's *heart* and *head* are better than common. He has a heart that prompts him to bless his people, and a head that directs him to the means.

Lilla. *(who has been looking out)* I see him Bendetta! I see him!

Bend. Where?

Lilla. There—there—what dont you know him

B

when you see him—have you forgotten his looks?

Bend. Dear, dear! at my age the eyes are not so sharp sighted as at your's—especialiy when love points out the object. Here they all come.

Vasq. Stand aside. Here. I go to attend my duty. (*exit* Vasquez, *after having placed the women near the wing. When* Lilla *sees* Rinaldo *enter, she points him out to* Bendetta. *Music.)*

enter ALPHONSO *and* CLARINDA; RINALDO *and* AL-ZAIRA; PEDRO, ISABELLA *and* CHILD; *ladies, who range themselves behind the characters; offi-cers and guards, who march up and down, rang-ing on each side and filling the stage. Music ceases.)*

Alph. It would have added to my happiness if your noble father could have honored my court and graced our nuptials with his presence.

Clar. How pleasing it would have been to his daughter's heart, I need not say, my lord; but eighty years must make his apology.

Rinald. The good old lord bade me to tell Al-phonso, that he sent him the better part of his heart, and in the remainder ever wore his image.

Alph. And his heart's better half shall enrich the bosom of Alphonso. O my loved brother, how much am I your debtor. How poor were all Al-phonso's treasures, lacking the diamond you have begged for him. But I will soon repay you. Al-zaira has consented to be your's to-morrow.

Rinald. Then shall I be royally repaid, my lord. Alzaira does not oppose the king's decree? (*she bows and gives her hand*) And you—(*to the child*) shall I be your father?

Child. O yes! the king told me you would.

Lilla. Come !—let us go ! Bendetta !

[*exit leaning on* Bendetta

Rinald. (*seeing* Lilla) Heavenly powers ! what do I see !

Alz. (*looking at* Rinaldo *and* Lilla) What is the matter, prince ?—you are disturbed—whom do you seek ?——(*hautboys without*)

Alph. What sounds are these, Alzaira ?

Alz. The neighboring peasants, my lord, wish to present their humble tokens of respect and loyalty to their queen. (*boats appear upon the river with peasants carrying flowers, garlands, &c. the masts of the boats are ornamented with garlands. When the boats are off the music ceases.*)

Clar My heart is full, my lord—you must teach me to repay your people love for love. I cannot express the satisfaction which these marks of approbation carry to my breast.

Alph. It shall be mine to reward my people for this token of their love and confidence.

(*music commences,* Alzaira *shows the bower, &c.*)

Clar. My heart will gratefully accept them.

Alzaira *shows the bower to* Alphonso, *who leads* Clarinda *thither, and they sit.* Rinaldo *and* Alzaira *are seated near the king ;* Rinaldo *appears troubled and scarcely attends to what passes.* Pedro, Isabella, *child and ladies, are on the side of the bower. Enter* VASQUEZ, *followed by peasants bearing baskets of fruit, they kneel before the king and queen, who take of the fruit,* Rinaldo *and* Alzaira, *the same ; and* Vasquez *and peasants range themselves behind ; during this, several young women and girls enter, immediately following* Vasquez, *with baskets of flowers and garlands, which they strew before the queen, form-ing a path of flowers from the bower. The child seeing this, runs up to a girl and takes a garland, with which he advances and offers it to the queen, who embraces him ; he then runs and places him-self on* Rinaldo's *knee. This is accompanied by music. Then follows—*

CHORUS.

Our humble off'ring thus we bring,
And thus with humble hearts we sing.
Hail to the happy, happy pair !
None but the good deserve the fair !

at the end of the chorus, the king rises, and leads Clarinda *forward,* Rinaldo *and* Alzaira, *&c. fol-lowing.*

Alph. Now let us on. Palermo is impatient to see her queen. Let me show to my beloved peo-ple, the gift that heaven has sent to make their father happy. (*trumpets. The king leads* Clarinda *off.* Rinaldo, Alzaira, *&c. follow, and as they are moving off to music, the curtain falls.*

END OF THE FIRST ACT.

✳

16

A C T   II.

SCENE—*the king's palace at Palermo.*

enter ALPHONSO *and* RINALDO.

Alph. O, Rinaldo, my brother, Clarinda far exceeds my utmost hopes; not only in external charms, but in those mental accomplishments—that cultivation of the mind and delicate sense of propriety, which must be the basis of my future happiness; for it is my ambition to show to my people an example of felicity in *that state* from which alone national prosperity can spring—the state of chaste and virtuous wedlock. You are silent, Rinaldo; the charms of Alzaira do not inspire you with rapture—nay, more, I can see that Alzaira has observed your coldness.

Rinald. I will hide nothing from you, my brother. In the garden of Oretto I saw a female, for whom my memory is deeply interested——for whom my heart cherishes ideas of the tenderest delight!

Alph. Who and what is she?

Rinald. Her name is Lilla, a peasant of the province of Bagaria, residing with a woman who was her nurse in her infancy. One day, when hunting in the neighborhood, I saw a lovely girl gathering flowers on the banks of a rivulet. I was charmed with her appearance. I often returned to see her. Her candor, her innocence, the frank avowal of her

B 2

love, all combined to inflame me—and passion annihilated reason—(Alphonso *is agitated*) soon after you called me to court. Occupied by the duties you entrusted to me, and carried away by the tide of daily occurrences, I could not return—though my heart oft reminded me of Lilla. She became a mother, and I learnt with grief, that her child lived but one day.

Alph. And you?

Rinald. My brother?

Alph. What did you do to repair these wrongs?

Rinald. I would have overwhelmed her with presents—but though often pressed she would accept of nothing from me.

Alph. Noble girl! and such is the being thou hast crushed!—riches!—presents!—thou didst rob her of her virgin affections—of her self-approbation—of her heart—of her worth—the very soul of her being—and offeredst in exchange thy gold!

Rinald. I feel my fault——

Alph. She rejected with disdain your presents, for she knew she had honestly purchased your heart—yes *honestly*, my brother—honestly paid the price you required—and all else appears worthless in her eyes. Such is the victim of your seduction. O, Rinaldo, my brother, I thought you without stain.

Rinald. Let my confession—my sincere contrition—my abhorrence of the crime, and determination to make amends, plead for me! and do you, my king, for I will not call you brother, assist me to cleanse this stain from my honor. O, God! who can conceive the torment of my soul, when, unexpectedly my eyes met the eyes of Lilla—when holding the hand of Alzaira as a pledge of union, Lilla, the injured Lilla, turned from me, wept and disappeared!

Alph. Yet Alzaira——

Rinald. I cannot think of an union with her, but with horror!

Alph. Her honor is *now* concerned; perhaps her heart. After proceeding almost to the altar——

Rinald. Torment on torment!—pardon me, my lord, it was in compliance with what I thought your wishes that I first turned my serious attentions towards Alzaira.

Alph. I knew not that you had other engagements. Besides, you appeared to seek the society of the beauteous widow——

Rinald. True, for a time her beauty blinded me; but even before my unexpected meeting with Lilla, I had remarked traits in the character of Alzaira which gave me little satisfaction. She has more of ambition than of tenderness in her composition: nay, even the most delicious feelings of nature seem strangers to her heart. Her lovely child, the admiration of all who see him, she views with indifference; whilst I feel an attachment to him stronger than reason can account for. I never see him but I say to myself such would have been the age of Lilla's child!

Alph. You are at this moment, a proof that no crime goes unpunished. Happy for you if your torments end here. You ought to fear that the supreme judge will one day call you to account for every tear you have caused to fall from the eyes of your innocent victim.

Rinald. Spare me, my lord! rather point out the way by which I shall regain my peace than add to my torments.

Alph. The way of virtue is the way of peace. I
will think how best I may extricate you from the
labyrinth of vice. In the mean time, although your
marriage with Alzaira is fixed for to-morrow, I will
take upon myself to delay it. Meanwhile, my brother, let this embarrassment teach you, that true
honor can only exist with perfect sincerity; and that
the higher our birth or fortune places us among
men, the more must we guard the propriety of our
actions, and scrutinize the purity of our intentions.
                                                            [*exit*

Rinald. Yes, I am the stain of nobility and
knighthood! I have planted a dagger in that innocent breast which duty and honor called upon me to
shield! poor unfortunate Lilla! what could have
brought her from her loved retirement?—to see her
betrayer once more?—once more to contemplate
the cause of all her woes?—o, that idea——heavens, what do I see!—it is herself—I dare not appear before her. (*retires back*)

        enter BENDETTA, LILLA *following timidly.*

Bend. Come child, what are you afraid of? this
is the place signora Isabella appointed. Hither she
promised to bring the boy, and when she comes you
can satisfy yourself and prove the truth or falsehood
of your suspicions; for you know—

Lilla. (*seeing* Rinaldo) Ah! come Bendetta!—

Rinald. (*approaching promptly*) Lilla!—you
here?—

Lilla. Pardon me my lord, I did not seek—I did
not expect to see you here. I fear my presence—
—I will retire——(*going*)

Rinald. Stop! pray stop, Lilla! it must have

been something highly interesting to you which could have drawn you hither. Let me not be an interruption to your designs ; but rather put it in my power to serve you. If you have any thing to ask from the king my brother, speak, and I pledge myself to obtain it.

Lilla. The king, your brother ! o, my lord ! why did you not earlier speak to me of the " king your brother ?"—then I had been safe, and now, perhaps happy.

Rinald. O pardon ! pardon me my Lilla ! I have been a deceiver ;—yet did I not deceive you more than myself. I have caused your precious tears to flow, and my heart has wept blood at the conviction. Believe me, Lilla, never did I love you more than at this moment, never did you appear so worthy of my love : and if it depended upon *my will* to make you happy, this moment should assure the felicity of your life.

Lilla. From the prince Rinaldo, I expect nothing: he can do nothing for the happiness of a poor cottager.

Rinald. If heaven had permitted him to live, I might at least have afforded that protection to the pledge of loves which his mother has refused.—

Lilla. Your son, my lord ! o, yes ! I believe you would have loved him. I saw you this morning caressing a child—if he should—(*aside*) o' delicious hope ! betray me not !——once more my lord permit me to assure you that I did not expect to see you here—I must retire.

Rinald. No Lilla, not so. You came here for some purpose which I interrupt—if we must part, it is my business to withdraw. (*takes her hand*) Lilla, the chain which unites our hearts is still unbro▾

ken! I conjure you, do not leave the palace—I must see you again!

Lilla Dearest Rinaldo—alas! forgive me, my lord—leave me prince—I pray you leave me!—I ought to forswear your presence forever.

Rinald. Heaven forbid! I will no longer interrupt your purpose of coming hither. I go to the king—I will—perhaps he—Lilla, nay dear Lilla! I conjure you to remain near the palace.   *[exit*

Lilla. O, Bendetta, my good Bendetta—scarce can I breathe—to see him, to hear the sound of his voice again! did you hear him? he called me his dear Lilla!

Bend. Yes, yes, that is the way they all talk. Do not you remember—but come come it will only put me in an ill humor. I wonder signora Isabella does not bring the boy. Indeed child those were strange things she told us of—marvellous circumstances! that the son of the lady Alzaira was scarcely living at its birth.

Lilla. And the story of the valet so skilful in simples who restored him to health so suddenly!

Bend. Ay, and the strong reasons from interest which she had—o, I have violent suspicions.

Lilla And you really noticed a mark upon the neck of the child?

Bend. Yes, just like the one I remember on your boy's neck.

Lilla. On the right side?

Bend. On the right side.

Lilla. If he has another smaller one on his left wrist, it is him, it is my son!

Bend. Alzaira lived sufficiently near us at the time—but here comes Isabella and the dear little boy. She has kept her word.

enter ISABELLA *and the* CHILD.

Lilla. Ah madam, how much you oblige me by your kindness—I have been impatient to see the child again. (*he runs to her with out-stretched arms, she kisses him, then eagerly examines his neck*) Yes, Bendetta, here is one of the marks!

Bend. Quick! seek for the second.

Lilla. O, let me breathe! I tremble—o no! such happiness cannot be in store for me! (*to Isabella*) I conjure you, madam, first tell me—let us take care, Bendetta: let me first ask this lady some questions, for I may learn from her, circumstances that will contradict the hopes these marks may raise, and then I shall sink from a moment of delusive joy, to grief ten times more cruel than that which inhabits my bosom.

Isab. From what I have imperfectly gathered, your story seems very extraordinary. I am sorry that I know no more of the circumstances which attended the event you are interested in : but the family of lord Bertoldo were at that time unknown to me. As to the child's being really the son of Alzaira, I never heard it doubted before.

Lilla Did the valet of whom you spoke, in reality possess such wonderful skill in simples : such power to restore health?

Isab. I know nothing of him but from report. This is certain, that he could not save himself from the stroke of death, for he expired suddenly a few days after the restoration of the child.

Lilla. Suddenly?—indeed?—

Bend. Did you ever learn his name?

Isab. I inquired, and they told me his name was Hospard.

Bend. Hospard ! we knew him well ; he had re-
lations close by us and often came to our house

Lilla. Can you tell us, madam, the precise time
that the child was born !

Isab. Yes, it was very remarkable, being the
very night of the last earthquake, when the flames
of Ætna were seen even in this part of the island.

Lilla. Heaven support me !

Bend. It is him, my Lilla ! (*presenting the child
to Lilla*) quick—seek the only proof that is want-
ing.

Lilla. (*trembles—hesitates and then uncovers his
wrist*) Look Bendetta ! it is ? it is my son ! (*embracing and kissing the child with vehemence*)

Bend. I was sure of it !

Isab. Can it be possible ?

Bend. There can be no doubt—every circumstance confirms it.

Lilla. He *is* my child——yet who will listen to
my story the complaint of the poor and unfriend-
ed ? the beatings of a mother's heart will not be
heard by my judges ! what proofs can I bring that
will avail against the power and the undisputed pre-
tentions of Alzaira?

Bend. You shall bring a thousand. But first, begin by taking possession of what is your own.
Justice is with us, then what have we to fear ? she
will complain to the king. So much the better :
the king is wise and good, and the righteous cause
is ours.

Lilla. O my boy ! come to my heart ! no, you
shall never part from me more ! Alphonso, on his
throne, will hear the complaint of a poor and injured
mother.

Isab. Alzaira comes!—heavens, what shall I say?

enter ALZAIRA.

Alz. (*seeing* Lilla *caressing the child.*) These women still here! Isabella, what do you do here with them? take the child and retire.

Isab. Madam, I tremble to tell you—these women—

Alz. These women! what have I to do with them? who gave them permission to enter the palace? good woman leave that child: you are too forward—

Lilla. (*firmly*) Madam, this child does not belong to you.

Alz. What do I hear!

Lilla. The truth.

Alz. What, is there a plot formed against me! a plot to rob me of my child! wretches! do you know who I am? do you know the punishment to which your insolence exposes you?

Lilla. At this moment, madam, I can only know —can only fell—one thing: that I am a mother: —that this is my child:—that he was stolen from me the night after his birth:—that I now recognize him by indubitable marks :—

Alz. How!—marks!

Berd. Yes, madam, and in your countenance one may at this moment see further proofs of what she asserts. You have not forgotten the hopeless state in which your child was born: you have not forgotten the miracle which was wrought by the convenient valet, Hospard.

c

Alz. Hospard !—*(recovering from her surprise and terror;* this is too much ! thus to be insulted and by wretches such as these ! for you, Isabella, dearly shall you pay this breach of trust. (*to* Lilla) Give me he child !

Lilla. (*embracing him*) My life as soon.

Alz. Guards ! (*enter soldiers*) arrest these daring women, who would by force carry off my son, even in the palace of their royal master. (*guards approach* Lilla)

Lilla. You are deceived (*to the soldiers*) he is mine ! I—I am his mother.

Bend. Carry us to the king ; he will do us justice. (*guards pause and retire back*)

Alz. What ! do you hesitate to obey me ? is there one of you that does not know the son of Bertoldo ? the son of your loved commander ! (*to Lilla*) wretched women, give me the boy. (*takes hold of the child*)

Lilla. Never, never !

Alz. In vain you struggle. (*Alzaira pulling the child forcibly Lilla yields him and Alzaira leads him to the other side*)

Bend. What do you give him up so easily ?

Lilla. I feared she would hurt him.

Alz. (*to Isabella*) Lead him in.

              [*exit* Isabella *and the child*

Lilla. (*following*) My child !

Alz. (*stopping her*) Stop !—guards, put these women out of the palace. (*soldiers advance between* Alzaira *and* Lilla)

Lilla. For pity ! for pity's sake let us see the king. He will not refuse to hear us.

Bend. We would speak to the king. (*guards retire on seeing Rinaldo*) *enter* RINALDO.

Rinald. What noise disturbs——you here madam ? (*to* Alzaira)

Lilla Heavens ! Rinaldo !

Alz. Prince, can you credit me when I say, they would rob me of my son ?

Bend. Not *her* son ? he is the son of Lilla !

Rinald. (*seeing* Lilla) What !—do you lay claim——

Alz. Think, prince Rinaldo, think of the unparalled audacity ! to pretend that my son is hers, stolen from her, she says when sleeping. I pray you my lord, order the guards to put this woman from the palace.

Lilla. Put me from the palace ! are you satisfied with so slight a punishment ? no, if I am guilty of wishing to deprive a mother of her child, I merit death !

Rinald. (*aside*) Can it be that I shall know such happiness—(*advancing to* Lilla) that boy—say you he is yours ?

Lilla. Yes, he is my son ! he is the fruit—(*checks herself*)——he is the son of a man, dear to my heart, but whom I ought not to name. Let the child be restored me, he is all that remains to me of the father.

Rinald. And do you accuse the lady Alzaira?

Lilla. I accuse no one. Her child died and they substituted mine in his place. Whether without her knowledge, or by her orders, I know not.

Rinald. Can it be possible !—does not some illusion mislead you ?—have you any proofs ?

Bend. Yes we have proofs sufficient. All we

ask is to be permitted to speak to the king ; but that the lady fears.

Rinald. (*scrutinizing* Alzaira) The lady fears you should speak to the king ?

Alz. I cannot but admire with what compaisance prince Rinaldo questions these women ; but I suspect a motive which will do him little honor. I remarked this morning the impression which the sight of this girl made upon him. You are quick sighted my lord, you can see, even under homely garments, charms which it is very difficult for another eye to discover.

Rinald. Madam, the question, now, concerns her misery, not her charms. It is possible that she deceives herself; it is possible that you may have been deceived. She must be heard. She claims the king's justice : and it is my duty to bring her before him.

Alz. What! upon the simple assertion of an unknown woman is Alzaira's honor to be questioned? me, who might presume upon some weight, some consideration, in the mind, if not in the heart, of Rinaldo! what! believe that of *me*, which nothing but the most positive proof ought to fix on the meanest wretch in creation!—can I believe my senses ?—is it Rinaldo speaks ?

Rinald. Why should we refuse to hear this woman ? is it because she is without protection ? you, madam, stand supported by your riches, and the revered name of your late illustrious lord ; she is without support—is she therefore not to be heard? no, madam, you better know what is due to yourself. Shall it be said that Alzaira feared the complaint of an unprotected cottager ? no, madam, *you*, doubtless, can silence *her* complaints before the throne of Alphonso.

Alz. Do not obliging think, great sir, that I feel the necessity of defending myself; nor imagine that I shall descend to the humiliating task, of publicly supporting my incontestable rights.

enter PEDRO.

Pedro. My lord, the king having heard of the dispute which has arisen concerning the child of the lady Alzaira, wishes to examine the business himself. To-morrow morning, on his return from solemnizing his nuptials, he will hear the cottage girl in the presence of Alzaira. It is the king's will, my lord, that you give the necessary orders for the execution of his purpose.

Lilla. (*aside*) Heaven be praised!

Rinald. Madam, you hear his majesty's will: your presence is absolutely necessary.

Alz. His majesty's will shall be obeyed. I will appear and triumph in the confusion which will overwhelm the object of your protection. Farewel my lord. (*casts a menacing look at* Lilla, *and is going*)

Pedro. One moment, madam: I have not yet fulfilled my commission to the prince. (*she returns*) It is the king's command that the child shall be conducted immediately to the lady Clarinda, where he will be tenderly protected, until the king's decision shall give him to his mother.

Rinald. (*eagerly*) Guards, instantly seek the boy! (*a soldier goes out*)

Alz. Do you think that I will suffer it? (*is following*)

Rinald. (*stopping her by taking her hand*) Stop

c 2

madam, what have *you* to fear ? are you not certain
that he will be returned to *you* ?

Alz. (*after a pause of confusion*) Tis well, Rinaldo—go on—display yourself ! (*to Lilla*) I congratulate you, madam, on the astonishing protection
you find at court. You need not doubt, my lord,
of becoming gratitude on her part. But let her
dread my vengeance ! what ? is the name of Bertoldo so soon forgotten ? let her dread the vengeance
of the relict of Bertoldo !

Lilla. Lady, if you repeat so loud a borrowed
name, a husband's name, I shall, perhaps, be tempted to make known my own.

Rinald. How !

Lilla. If names are to have weight in the scales
of justice, I can pronounce a father's name untaint-
ed in the rolls of honor.

enter GUARD, ISABELLA *and* CHILD.

(*as they pass from behind,* Alzaira *makes a motion as if
to take the child, the soldier places himself between
them*)

Lilla. (*on the first motion of* Alzaira *cries out*)
Hold ! !

Rinald. (*to* Alzaira, *as he takes the child*) Permit
me, madam. (*brings the child forward to front, ex-
amining and comparing him with* Lilla)

Alz. Still better, my lord ! why not proceed ?
why do you not give the child to my worthy rival ?

Rinald. No, madam, that would be doing injustice : and notwithstanding the opinion you have
formed of my conduct, I am innocent of injustice
towards *you*. Come, my sweet boy ; you have nothing to fear with me.

Lilla. (*with transport*) No, indeed. In your arms, he is——

Rinald. (*alarmed*) What say you ?——

Lilla. (*restraining her emotion*) O, my lord, the carresses bestowed on her child sink deep in a mother's heart.

Rinald. Is he indeed your son ?

Lilla Yes, a son torn from me by the cruel hand——but enough.—let the king hear me !

Rinald. What proof have you ?

Lilla. 'Tis here (*pointing to her heart*)——the angel is my own.

Rinald. Dare you maintain your claim before the king ?

Lilla. Yes, before my God.

Rinald. (*aside looking at the child*) Lovely boy ! should you prove—(*checks himself and turns to the guards*) on peril of your lives, watch over the welfare of this woman, and let nothing prevent her appearing before the king to-morrow ; (*takes the hand of the child*) come Pedro, let us place this precious deposit in the hands of the lady Clarinda. (*to* Lilla) You, madam, have no fear in confiding him to my care.

Lilla. I am satisfied, my lord.

Alz. Her triumph will be short. Alphonso will not see with the eyes of Rinaldo.

Rinald. Be assured, madam, that no means of discovering the truth will be neglected, either by Alphonso or Rinaldo. (*he leads the child up the stage. followed by* Pedro *and* Isabella)

Alz. I fear it not !   [*exit*
(*the guards,* Lilla *and* Bendetta *go off ;* Lilla *turning and looking at the child until he is no more to be seen.*

END OF THE SECOND ACT.

A C T   III.

SCENE—*the hall of the palace.   A throne, canopy,*
seats, &c.

enter RINALDO *and* PEDRO.

Rinald. Yes, noble Pedro, if Lilla is the mother
of the boy, I am his father.   My fate hangs upon
the approaching moment and my soul is impatient for the decision.   I left Alphonso and Clarinda at the altar that I might see again the good
Bendetta,   and make her repeat again and again
each circumstance that is allied to this dark trans-
action.   There are no positive proofs. it is true—
but I know the heart of Lilla, it is void of all ar-
tifice.   If the child is not hers, she is deceived,
for she is incapable of deceiving.

Pedro. Has the boy any resemblance to either
of the claimants ?

Rinald. I examined his lovely face to-day—yes,
Pedro,   his features are the features of Lilla.
When he smiled, I could have sworn it was the
smile of my Lilla !

Pedro. Be cautious, my lord, how you yield to
the illusion of hope.   In obedience to the king's
orders,   I have examined the servants and fol-
lowers of Alzaira, but I must confess I can gain
no intelligence that would flatter your wishes.

Rinald. But the testimony of Bendetta.

Pedro. It would have weight but from her connection with Lilla, which nearly puts it aside. All the wisdom of our sovereign will scarcely suffice to bring forth the truth.

Rinald. The truth will be made known, justice will prevail!—but hark—(*distant shouts*) they have left the cathedral of St. Rosalia.

Pedro. Yes, the august ceremony is over. The king and queen will return now to the palace and here receive the congratulations of their people. Then, immediately, will this extraordinary appeal be heard, and Alphonso pronounce the dictates of wisdom and justice.

Rinald. Which will be the triumph of nature and virtue.

Pedro. If Alzaira is proved guilty of this crime, you, my lord, will not think of marrying her?

Rinald. Marry her! marry Alzaira! no——though she should triumph before the judgment seat of Alphonso, there is a secret voice in my breast that will condemn her. (*noise approaches, music is heard*) They come! heavens! what a moment for my heart!—if Alzaira triumphs, the dearest illusion of my life will have vanished: but if the child is restored to Lilla, I shall press my son in my arms, and seek through life, to make amends to his lovely mother!

(*trumpets, music.*)

Enter guards ; then ALPHONSO *and* CLARINDA, *gentlemen and ladies.* RINALDO *congratulates the royal pair.* ALPHONSO *leads* CLARINDA *to the throne and they seat themselves,* RINALDO *on one side,* PEDRO *on the other. Enter young women*

*and girls.   Enter young men who range in front
of the guards : they enter singing the following*

CHORUS.

*Powers supreme, who love the just !
Now ope, of good. your endless store.
Powers of heaven in whom we trust !
Your blessings on our sov'reigns pour !*

SOLO, *by a young woman.*

*Long may Alphonso's wisdom bless,
   The people in whose hearts he reigns !
The injured here shall find redress,
   Where power to hear the lowly deigns.*
                         CHORUS. Powers, &c. &c.

Alph. (*descends from the throne leading the queen*)
Now, my beloved, my queen, my bride ! while
duty here detains me, go, surrounded by your people and covered by their blessings, go—and with
a hand as liberal as your heart, make Sicily acknowledge to her extremest borders, the bounty of
heaven, in sending her Clarinda, as her queen.

Clar. My lord, knowing that the happiness of your
people is your happiness, I shall study to please you
by blessing them.
   [*exit* Clarinda.   *Trumpets sound. The ladies, young
      women, girls and young men follow*

Alph. I hope, Rinaldo, we shall now soon know,
whether Alzaira is worthy of becoming your bride.

Rinald. O, my lord, speak not of Alzaira : the
mother of the boy can alone be the bride of Rinaldo.

Alph. And if Alzaira is the mother?

Rinald. Alzaira! no, the woman who loves not her child, is no mother.

Alph. You are very prompt in condemning her. Have you gained any other information more than Pedro has reported to me?

Rinald. No, my lord.

Alph. And without proof, merely on presump-tion, because your wishes are for Lilla, must Al-zaira be pronounced guilty! o, my brother. it is not by our feelings, our affections, our partialities, that we must judge of human actions. Justice, that sublime attribute of the godhead, ought to be pure as the source from whence it emanates. Per-haps I wish as much as you, that Lilla may restore a son to the arms of his father; but let us dread the possibility of forcing a child from the bosom of his mother: here an error would be a crime. But it is time to hear the contending mothers. Let them be brought hither. (*two soldiers go out opposite sides. Kneels.*) God of our fathers, crea-tor of the universe! let a ray of thy divine wis-dom fall upon my soul! assist me to dispel those clouds which envelope truth, that her brightness may shine to conviction!—o, suffer not, in the judgment I shall pronounce, suffer not the words of injustice to pass my lips. (*rises*) As to you, my brother, that your feelings may not mislead you, I command on your part absolute silence.

Alphonso *seats himself on the throne,* Rinaldo *and* Pedro *are seated near him.* ALZAIRA *enters, she bows slightly and haughtily to the king.* LILLA *enters, followed by* BENDETTA; *she advances modestly, and bows lowly before the throne, then retires: seats are placed for the women on the sides they entered.*

Alph. Lilla, you claim as your child, one whom Alzaira, the widow of the lord Bertoldo, has always declared to be her son. Speak, tell us who you are, and by what proofs you support your claim. Lady Alzaira, pray you be seated.

(Alzaira *sits*)

Lilla. In this august presence, humbly, yet firmly, I attest that being who reads all hearts, that my lips shall only utter the dictates of truth. My lord, I am the daughter of the count Gradina, who died fighting for his country.

Rinald. The daughter of Gradina !

Alph. He was a brave soldier !

Lilla. Condemned to poverty by the cruel fate of war, I passed my days in tranquillity and obscurity on the banks of the Bagaria, in the cottage of the good Bendetta. There I was content, and should still have been, but for the love—give me leave, great king, to pass over the time until the period when it pleased heaven to permit that I should become a mother. It was on that memorable night, three years ago, when Ætna shook our island to its foundation. I clasped my boy with transport to my bosom, no fears for his life once entered my thoughts, for health bloomed upon his visage. Judge my despair at awaking next morning, to find in his place a strange child, cold, pale, dead! vain were my tears and complaints —the dead child passed for mine. It was not until yesterday that I learned that a very different scene passed at the same hour in the chamber of the lady Alzaira, who then with her noble lord, dwelt in Bagaria.

Alph. Was your child born at that period, my lady ?

Alz. Yes, my lord, he was.

Lilia. Feeble was he born and scarcely living. A servant of the name of Hospard, who knew us and all our affairs perfectly, suddenly left lord Bertoldo's house and appeared again in the morning; at which time the cradle of the dying child offered to the eyes of the astonished attendants, a child full of strength and health. O, great king, does not such a strange concurrence of circumstances carry conviction to your soul? o, give credit to the heart of a mother which nature cannot deceive! every feature of a child, every mark, imperceptible to indifferent eyes, are indelibly imprinted upon a mother's heart. Two marks were placed by nature upon my son. Yesterday I met the reputed child of Alzaira; my heart was moved; I examined his features; my emotion increased: I saw the two signs; the light burst upon me: my heart cried aloud, " You hold your son in your arms "

Alph. Were the marks of which you speak, observed by any other person at the time?

Bend. Yes, my lord, I noted them.

Alph. You are—?

Lilla She is my friend, benefactor, mother?

Alph. Did any other person note them?

Lilla. No, my lord.

Alph. And Hospard?

Bend. Is dead, my lord. But what proofs do we want? the children born at the same time! Hospard's departure from home—his knowledge of us—besides, my lord, how easy to enter our humble cottage while we slept—the habitations of the poor have neither locks nor bars to secure them.

Alph. Alzaira, are the circumstances they mention, concerning the birth of your infant, true?

D

Alz. (*rising*) They are, my lord. But what con-
clusion can be drawn from events so natural ? my
son, it is true, had need of quick and powerful aid,
and he found it.—Hospard, skilled in the properties
of healing plants, flew to search the neighboring
country, and his zeal was crowned by success.
What is there astonishing in this ? what is it to me
whether or not a child was stolen from an obscure
hovel on the banks of the Bagaria ? but what proofs
are there of such an event ? who will vouch that the
child found dead in yon woman's cradle was not her
child ? you have *her* word for it, and that of her ac-
complice ! and in respect to the natural marks,
who saw any such on her child ! truly, the same unim-
peachable testimony !—it is strange, inconceivably
strange, that when all Sicily can bear witness in my
favor, and testify my indisputed right to my child,
so absurd, so ridiculous a complaint should be made
for a moment the subject of attention, or bring me
into comparison with such people.

Lilla. Madam, the more my claims appear absurd, ridiculous and extraordinary, the more should
be the persuasion, that a poor unfortunate woman
would not dare to make an appeal to her sovereign,
without the most perfect conviction of the justice of
her cause.

Alz. Your suppositions should at least bear the
semblance of probability.

Lilla. Probability ! is it, then, improbable, madam, that you would be greatly interested in presenting a son to lord Bertoldo, when tis well known
that on that alone you depended to save you from
the shame of divorce ? but I am willing to believe
that you were ignorant of that crime which a friendly hand perpetrated for your service.   Yet, even

then, the voice of nature, which is never silent in the heart of a mother, ought to have given you sufficient notice, that you had no part in the child you did not love.

Alz. Who has said that I never loved my son?

Lilla. All those who know you.

Alz. My lord, since injurious treatment is substituted instead of proofs, I pray you pronounce judgment. I wish to have my son restored to me.

Alph. Bring the child hither.   [*exit a soldier*

Lilla. O, Bendetta! what is to be my fate!

re-enter soldier with the child.

Alph. My brother receive the boy. (*the child is led to* Rinaldo.) Alzaira and Lilla, how can I safely pronounce judgment between you. The one has in her favor long established possession, unquestioned until this day; but her right is now contested, if not with proofs, at least with presumptions, which are advanced with an air of truth that give them double force. I see nothing but doubt and obscurity; if I give the infant to one, I perhaps deprive the other of her child: while it is possible that there is no guilt on either part, and that she who in reality is not the mother, believes herself to be so. Let one of you make a generous effort in favor of her rival; and I promise to exert my utmost power to make her recompense.

Lilla. O, my lord! the treasures of your kingdom would not pay me for the sacrifice of my child.

Alph. Alzaira, what say you?

Alz. Give him up to that woman! no! rather would I see him perish.

Alph. Perish! (*reflects a moment*) the ray of light has fallen!---since neither will yield to the other, listen to the irrevocable sentence which I shall pronounce. My lord Pedro.----a tablet and pencil. (*it is brought; the king writes quickly a few words*)

Rinald. My brother!------

Alph. Read. (Rinaldo *reads, then satisfied returns the tablet*) Execute this order. (*gives the tablet to a soldier. Exit soldier.*) Alzaira, your words have determined me. It is better to weep over the ashes of a beloved child, than to see it living in the power of a detested rival.

the soldier re-enters, followed by an executioner, his sleeves rolled up, and a sword in his hand.

Take that child: let him die; and let his remains be gathered into two distinct tombs, one for each mother. (*the executioner seizes the boy, who kneels, supplicating*)

Lilla. No, great king! you will not order so barbarous a deed!

Alph. Take him from the presence, and execute my orders.

Child. Oh! don't hurt me. (*they are leading him off*)

Lilla. Hold! hold! let him live---let Alzaira take him---but let him live! (*rushing forward, and prostrating herself*)

Alph. (*descends from his throne rapidly, and comes forward*) Nature has spoken. Behold the mother! give the child to Lilla---the voice of nature cannot err. (*the child is led to* Lilla)

Lilla. (*rising and pressing him to her bosom*) Have I my child! yes, yes, I am a mother!

Rinald. Daughter of Gradina, Lilla, my dear Lilla! you are not alone in this joy! come, my boy, come to the arms of a father! (*embracing him*)

Alz. What do I hear ?---Rinaldo!

Rinald. Yes, he is my son---his mother my wife!

Alz. I acknowledge the justness of my punishment, o, father of mercies, and sink before that eye which cannot be deceived! (*kneels to the king*) My lord, your wisdom has unveiled my crime, and an unseen power forces from my lips a full confession! yes, I have sinned against the voice of nature! I have belied the purity of nature---in calling myself a mother, and consenting to the death of my child!

Alph. Alzaira, in consideration of this declaration, I will not pronounce that sentence upon you which your crime merits. But retire from Palermo, repent and live to virtue.

Alz. I acknowledge your mercy, as well as your justice. (*she bows---bursts into tears, and exit*)

Alph. To-morrow, my brother, you shall be united to Lilla. I will be present with my court at the solemnity. We will do all that remains in our power to make amends for the past, and to do honor to the virtues of Lilla, and to the voice of nature.

END OF VOICE OF NATURE.

EPILOGUE.

WRITTEN BY WILLIAM DUNLAP,

Spoken by Mrs. Johnson.

So, I have played Alzaira's part quite through—
But is it drawn from nature?—— is it true?
Could any female who had ever known,
E'er felt, a mother's anguish as her own,
Conceive the thought of tearing from her breast
The joy that lulls a mother's pains o rest?
O no, ! the libel never shall be believed ;
The thought was by unfeeling *man* conceived—
Man takes the pen, and as his passion sways,
Sketches, in harsh, coarse lines mild nature's
    ways ; .
Or, from his own dark breast combines hard fea-
    tures,—
Then, swears the ugly brat, is mother nature's.
  So, Shakspeare, when by moody humors
    sway'd—
When hags, and demons, 'fore his fancy played,
His mind familiar grown with blood and death,
Drew the cursed wife of wavering Macbeth.
  But do such things exist ?—I'll ne'er believe it !
Ladies I'm sure your minds can ne'er conceive it !
The *voice of nature*, is alive in all :
Your hearts have heard and answered to her call ;
The *female* heart, is, by the will of heaven,
To nature, as her sacred temple, given ;

And when this truth is falsified by *man*,
It is a libel on creation's plan.
   Alzaira ——though I believe the poet drew
The story from a source acknowledged true——
Is so at variance with the female heart
That mine *revolts whene'er I read the part;*
So, ladies, if I play without due spirit,
You must not place it to my heart s demerit.
I am a mother——can I represent
One who could steal the mother's best content ;
Rob from the parent breast her darling bliss ;—
O, no !—I cannot feel a part like this !
Yet well I know it is the drama's task,
To tear from vice her highly polished mask ;
And she who makes guilt hateful, serves the
   cause.
Of virtue, and deserves as much applause,
As one, who robed in truth's eternal rays,
Persuades to tread her ever-pleasant ways.
Armed with this thought, for you I'll do my best,
To represent a being——*I detest.*
   There was a time, when ladies, though they
   felt
Fair nature's voice, and at her altars knelt ;
Yet, like some devotees, of whom tis said
That to appear religious is their dread——
They kept their true devotion in the heart,
And *seem'd* to worship nature's *rival*, art :
Their locks, which nature bade in ringlets flow,
Were upright reared, a monument of woe ;
Their necks, where every grace enthroned ap-
   pears,
Were ruffed all 'round, and kerchiefed to the ears;

All fair proportion from the form was driven,
And stays, and hoops, belied the work of heaven.
   But,—taste be thanked!---that time is now long
     past;
The *voice of nature* has been heard at last:
Each female, gladly, nature's call obeys,
And doffs her ruffs, her kerchiefs, and her stays,
Her hoops, her pockets---all are laid aside,
And beauty boasts that *nature* is her pride.
   Long may that beauty which this presence
     graces——
Assemblage sweet, of joy illumined faces——
Where every form and every lovely feature,
Bespeaks attention to the *voice of nature*.---
Enjoy those blessings which from virtue flow,
Health unalloyed, and *bliss* unmixed with woe!

✳

THE
VOICE OF NATURE

Incidental Music to the Play

by

WILLIAM DUNLAP

Composed by

VICTOR PELISSIER

(1803)

Reconstructed and edited from manuscript parts in the

New York Public Library

Music Division

by

KARL KROEGER

No.1 March

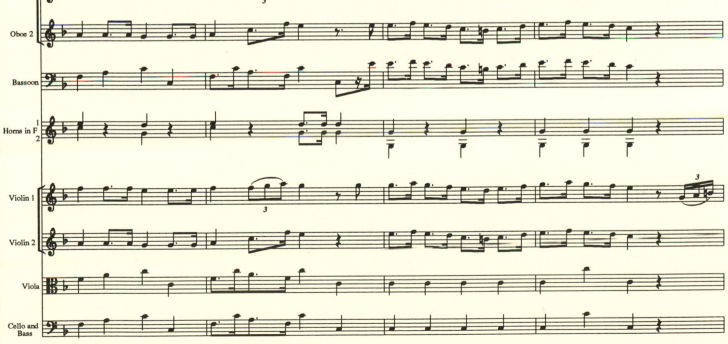

48

51

No.2

No.3 March and Chorus

Allegretto

57

Chorus

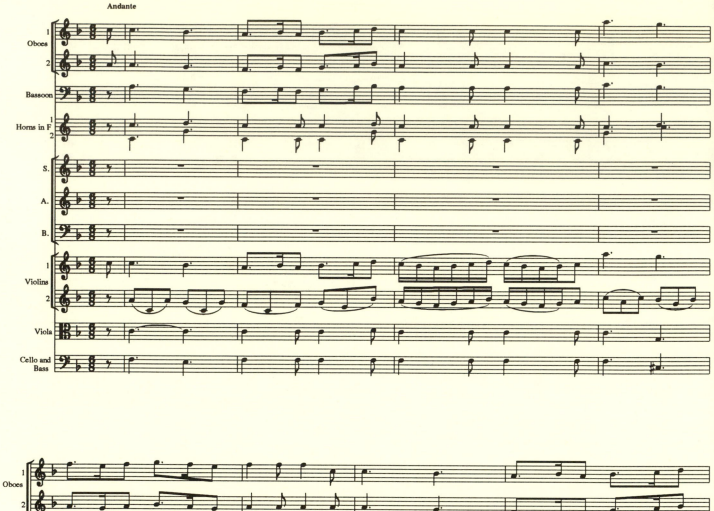

Our hum - ble off' - rings thus _____ we

Our hum - ble off' - rings thus _____ we

Our hum - ble off' - rings thus we

bring,   and thus with hum - ble hearts we sing;

bring,   and thus with hum - ble hearts we sing;

bring,   and thus with hum - ble hearts we sing;

Hail to the hap - py, hap - py pair! None but the good de - serve the fair!

Hail to the hap - py hap - py pair! None but the good de - serve the fair!

Hail to the hap - py hap - py pair! None but the good de - serve ___ the fair!

None but the good ___ de - serve ___ the fair! De - serve the fair! ___ De -

None but the good ___ de - serve ___ the fair! De - serve the fair! ___ De

None but the good ___ de - serve ___ the fair! De - serve the fair! ___ De -

serve the fair! ___ None

serve the fair! ___ None but the good ___

serve the fair! ___ None but the good ___

61

66

No.4 MARCH and CHORUS

68

Chorus

71

72

on　　　　our　　　　sove　-　　　　reigns　　　　pour!

on　　　　our　　　　sove　-　　　　reigns　　　　pour!

on　　　　our　　　　sove　-　　　　reigns　　　　pour!

on　　　our　　　sove　-　　　reigns　　　pour!

on　　　our　　　sove　-　　　reigns　　　pour!

on　　　our　　　sove　-　　　reigns　　　pour!

75

in whose heart he reigns _____ the in - jured _____ here _____ shall find _____ re -

dress _____ where power _____ to _____ hear _____ the low - ly

deigns _____ where power _____ to

hear _____ the low ly deigns.

78

The Aethiop; or,
The Child of the Desert

Drawn by Bennett — Engraved by Freeman

William Dimond, Esq.

CAST OF CHARACTERS

The Aethiop (Haroun Al-Raschid, Caliph of Baghdad)..........................Speaker

Almanzor, an Arabian sage and chief conspirator...............................Speaker

Orasmyn, his nephew and pretender to the throne (Child
 of the Desert)..Speaker

Giafar, Al-Raschid's vizier...Speaker

Nourreddin, Giafar's lieutenant..Bass

Abdallah, an iman..Speaker

Aladin..Speaker

Sentinel..Speaker

Caled, Almanzor's slave..Speaker

Cephania, Al-Raschid's Queen and Orasmin's sister.........................Speaker

Immyne, Cephania's lady-in-waiting...Speaker

* * *

Alexis, young Greek Christian resident of Baghdad............................Baritone

Benmoussaff, a cadi...Tenor

Mustapha, an emir...Speaker

Zoe, Alexis's wife..Soprano

Constantine, Alexis's cousin...Speaker

Grimnigra, Mustapha's wife..Speaker

Grumnildra, Benmoussaff's wife..Speaker

An Old Woman...Speaker

Citizens of Baghdad; conspirators...Chorus SATB

Turkish Guards

Corps de Ballet, Cephania's attendants

* * *

INSTRUMENTS OF THE ORCHESTRA

2 Flutes (and Piccolo)

2 Oboes

2 Clarinets (in B-flat, C)

2 Bassoons

2 Horns (in C, D, E-flat, F, G, A)

2 Trumpets (in C, E-flat, F, A)

2 Timpani (in C, D, E, F, G, A)

Bass Drum

Snare Drum

Cymbals

Triangle (or Cow Bell)

Violins 1

Violins 2

Violas

Violoncellos

Contrabasses

The first performance of the Taylor-Yellin restoration of *The Aethiop* by The Federal Music Society took place at Town Hall, New York on May 18, 1978.

Orchestral parts are available from The Federal Music Society, Frederick R. Selch, President, 132 East 71st Street, New York, NY 10021.

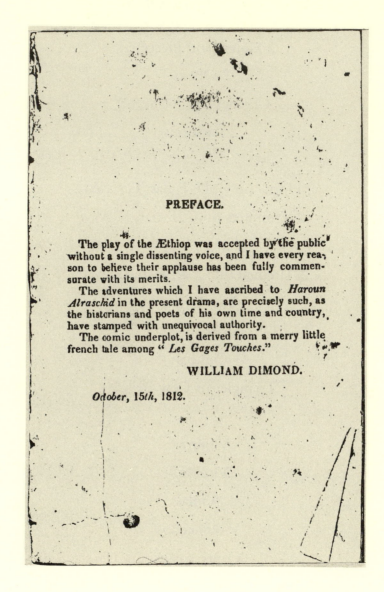

PREFACE.

The play of the Æthiop was accepted by the public without a single dissenting voice, and I have every reason to believe their applause has been fully commensurate with its merits.

The adventures which I have ascribed to *Haroun Alraschid* in the present drama, are precisely such, as the historians and poets of his own time and country, have stamped with unequivocal authority.

The comic underplot, is derived from a merry little french tale among " *Les Gages Touches.*"

WILLIAM DIMOND.

October, 15th, 1812.

THE ÆTHIOP;

OR,

THE CHILD OF THE DESERT;

A ROMANTIC PLAY,

IN THREE ACTS.

—◆—

BY WILLIAM DIMOND;

AUTHOR OF "HUNTER OF THE ALPS,"—"ADRIAN
AND ORRILA,"—"HERO OF THE NORTH,"
—"PEASANT BOY," &c. &c.

—◆—

[from the first London edition, of 1812.]

———

NEW-YORK:

PUBLISHED BY D. LONGWORTH,
At the Dramatic Repository,
Shakspeare-Gallery.

—◆—

March.—1813.

DRAMATIS PERSONÆ.

Covent-garden.

The Æthiop,	Mr. C. Kemble,
Almanzor, an arabian sage,	— Young,
Orasmyn, nephew to Almanzor,	— Booth,
Giafar, a vizier,	— Egerton,
Nourreddin,	— Duruset,
Aladin,	— Treby,
Caled, an arab slave,	— Jefferies,
Mustapha, an emir,	— Simmons,
Benmoussaff, a cadi,	— Liston,
Alexis, } greek christians,	— Fawcett,
Constantine, }	— Broadhurst,
Cephania, niece to Almanzor, and wife to the caliph,	Mrs. H. Johnstone,
Immyne,	Miss Logan,
Grimnigra, wife to Mustapha,	Mrs. Davenport,
Grumnildra, wife to Benmoussaff,	Miss Leserve,
Zoe, wife to Alexis,	Mrs. C. Kemble,

SCENÉ—Bagdat.

The music by mr. Bishop.

THE ÆTHIOP;

OR,

THE CHILD OF THE DESERT.

ACT I.

SCENE 1—*a spacious terrace in front of the seraglio, overlooking the river Tigris, the opposite bank of which is seen at a distance, crowned with mosques and minarets—the gate of the palace opens, and several guards rush forth confusedly dragging forward a sentinel—an officer follows, who in one hand holds a scroll, and with the other menaces the sentinel—citizens of Bagdat, male and female, enter from all sides and surround the tumult with expressions of curiosity.*

CHORUS.

Nour.	Speak, caitiff, speak ! what hand profane
	Yon walls with treason dared to stain——
	Who traced this scroll ? who placed it there ?
	His name pronounce—his haunt declare !
Sent.	I'm innocent.—I know no more——
Off.	Die ! traitor, die !
Sent.	I kneel—implore !
Citizens.	Ah ! whence this rage ? why shakes that slave ?
	And what portends yon scroll, we crave ?
Nour.	A plot against the caliph's throne——
	Speak, perjured slave ! thy treasons own !
Sent.	I'm innocent, by heaven ! I swear——
All.	To rack and fire the traitor bear !

B

GIAFAR *descends the terrace.*

Giaf. How now ! Nourreddin—whence this tumult ? even at the palace gate.

Nour. Illustrious Giafar ! behold this traitor and pronounce his doom. The western quadrangle of the palace this hour was his allotted watch, and now within its sacred precinct is this scroll discovered.

Giaf. (*unfolds it*) Ha ! what characters are these ? by hell ! the well know cypher of the fallen *Ali !* (*reads*) " People of Bagdat ! rejoice ! the hour of your deliv- " erance is nigh. Death to Haroun Alraschid—victo- " ry to the race of Ali, the only true believers !" detested treason ! wretch ! if racks can rend——

Sent. Giafar ! our caliph's chosen counsellor ! less dreaded for thy power, than reverenced for thy virtues ; deign to regard and trust thy kneeling slave ! by allah and the blessed tomb ! I swear—my watch hath faithfully been kept. No stranger's step hath crossed its limit—the caliph's best loved confidants alone have passed.

Nour. Yet to the centre pillar of the quadrangle, the scroll was fixed. Vizier ! pronounce his sentence—the torture quickly shall extort the truth !

Giaf. Nourreddin ! hold—let justice be severe, yet not precipitate—guard the suspected man, but forbear his life.

enter an IMAN *through the crowd.*

Iman. Where is the vizier ? conduct me to his presence.

Giaf. Abdallah ! why hast thou left the mosque ? are the holy rites so soon concluded ?

Iman. A pious horror shakes my aged frame. Alas ! the blasphemy of traitors hath transgressed the very sanctuary of our faith. Even now, before our altar the sultana knelt and offered vows for great Alraschid's safety ! lo from the body of the shrine a voice replied, " woman, thy prayer is vain ! the child of the desert shall reclaim his own !"

Giaf. Immortal prophet!—the palace and the mosque at once profaned! speak! what followed?

Iman. Consternation seized on all the listening crowd—the trembling priesthood left their rites unfinished—and now in terror the sultana hastens from the mosque.

Giaf. Allah! preserve the caliph! father of mercies! guard thine image upon earth!

Iman. To this report let stranger words be joined—in the old burial place of Ali's sect—a cursed ground—which good men's feet even by day avoid—at the dead hour of night, wild music hath been heard to float, and wandering torches have been seen to glide; if e'er some curious step approached to search the wonder, instant the chant was hushed, and each small fire would vanish.

Giaf. The times are peril fraught—but holy friend, learn we to meet their temper with an even courage. Nourreddin! to thy especial charge this evening I confide the city—at each gate let the guard be doubled, and see it straight proclaimed through Bagdat, that every citizen retire within his house at sun-set, and under pain of death, drive forth all strangers from his door. *(music sounds from the river)* Hark! the sultana's galley!

Nour. Returning from the mosque upon the Tigris' further bank, the glittering barque now cleaves the stream. *(music renewed—the galley rows in sight—guards form in lines before the palace gate—the people cluster about—an arab with an agitated air, advances from amidst the crowd)*

Arab. Now comes the moment to discharge my trust. *(he accosts a citizen)* Friend, will not the sultana return into the palace by this gate?

Cit. Assuredly. Therefore tis, the citizens thus throng to pay their homage.

Arab. Acquaint me, I beseech, which is the fitting post for such as would present petitions?

Cit. Here, to the left—some suitors are already stationed. When the sultana passes, kneel with the others and extend your paper.

Arab. Thanks for your counsel.

Giaf. (*to Nourreddin*) Mark yon stranger!— he who struggles now to reach the gate—his gestures are confused.

Nour. His garb bespeaks him of the desert—he sees that you observe him, and avoids your eye.

Giaf. (*aloud*) Arab! come forward. Would'st thou petition the sultana?

Arab. Yea, mighty Giafar! my boon is trifling, yet have I travelled far to crave it.

Giaf. Declare to me its purport.

Arab. Simply, the sultana's protection for merchants of our tribe, who fain would trade with Bagdat.

Giaf. 'Tis well—guards! make way for the stranger. Look that he approach the sultana freely.

Arab. I kiss the dust before your feet in homage. (*as the arab bends, a paper, unperceived by him, falls at Giafar's foot—a guard raises it*)

Giaf. Hold! you have dropped a paper—is it your petition?

Arab. (*starting wildly*) Ha! yes, yes—give it me— restore it——

Giaf. Such eagerness! give *me* the paper!

Arab. Distraction! ruin!

Giaf. (*glancing his eye over the contents*) Eternal providence! seize on that discovered fiend! (*guards surround the arab—shouts sound from the water-side*) the sultana lands—drag him aside! swift! swift! this way—follow me! (*Giafar rapidly darts down a colonnade—the arab is dragged after by guards—the prow of the galley presents itself upon the stage—*CEPHANIA *appears seated in state—surrounded by her women and pages*)

CHORUS.

Queen of the east! whose beauty
Kills envy with its blaze—
Thy slaves in pleasing duty,
Aspire to sing thy praise.

Live, of our earth the wonder !
While thou dost grace our sphere,
E'en gods might quit their thunder
To kneel in homage here !

(in the course of the chorus the SULTANA *descends—the different petitioners kneel—she receives their papers graciously, then passes them to her principal woman—*GIAFAR *returns as the chorus closes, leading forward the arab)*

Giaf. Now, slave, kneel and present thy paper—ay ! that *very* paper !

Arab. Mercy ! mercy !

Giaf. Obey ! nay not one sign—or instant death.

Arab. Wretch that I am ! it must be so. (*he approaches Cephania—kneels with averted eyes, and silently extends the paper*)

Ceph. (*as she receives it*) Good fellow ! why dost thou tremble ? trust me, thy suit shall meet regard.

Arab. Ah ! sultana——

Giaf. (*interrupting*) The lustre of Cephania's eye hath dazzled monarchs—wherefore should she wonder that it awes a slave ? Nourreddin ! do thou conduct the stranger through the outer gates—(*aside*)—mark me —the deepest dungeon.

Arab. One word—one——

Giaf. (*aside in a low menacing tone*) Silence ! or thy death is instant.

Arab. Lost ! lost ! our cause is lost for ever !

[*exit with guards, gazing to the last upon Cephania*

Ceph. Giafar ! how earnestly did that poor arab fix his eyes on mine at parting ! surely no common suit could move him thus—Immyne ! preserve his paper separate from the rest, and let me read it when I reach my chamber.

Giaf. Queen of the east ! the caliph watches your return from mosque, and trusts a prosperous omen crowns your vows.

Ceph. The mosque ! ah, Giafar—a fatal augury requites my prayer—but hence with ill-divining thoughts !

B 2

Alraschid's wife should scorn their influence—the heavens will guard their own—I bless the prophet, and defy my fate!

CHORUS.

Queen of the east, whose beauty, &c.

(Cephania ascends the terrace to the seraglio gate, followed by her train—the people prostrate themselves as she passes—the scene closes on the group)

SCENE II—*inside of Alexis's cabin.*

enter ZOE.

Zoe. Alexis! Alexis! renegade bridegroom of mine! whither wander you? you left me before sun rise to drive the camel toward the desert, and twelve long, *long* hours have wasted since in solitude. There all the city has been making holyday, to see the sultana, and hear the fine music on the Tigris—yet Zoe must keep house the while! ah! for this fond heart! the court pageant and its minstrelsy, passed unseen—unheard—for Alexis paced the desert, and watchful Zoe, could only listen for his camel's bell!

AIR—ZOE.

From twining arms, ere sun rise starting,
    Alexis sigh'd a fond farewell,
And as we pledged a kiss at parting
    He bade me watch the *camel's bell.*
Sweet ding, ding, dong! I heard it play—
Methought its jingle seem'd to say
" With burning noon will come the time
Again to hear my pleasant chime !"
        O! cheerful bell!
        I loved thee well,
And still to break my lonely song
'Thy changes rang with ding, ding, dong!

But noon hath pass'd, twelve hours have fleeted—
    Since last Alexis bade adieu!

My watch is vain—my hopes are cheated—
    And now I deem the bell untrue,
Its jingle still I strive to hear—
But silence mocks my wishful ear,
Ah ! when shall come the promised time
Once more to hear that pleasant chime?
        Dear, faithless bell !
        I prithee tell—
And sweetly close my lonely song
With changes rang of ding, ding, dong !

        (*a soft tap is given against the door*)

Zoe. Ah ! there's somebody at the door—tis surely Alexis—how delightful ! (*opens it, and* BENMOUSSAFF *enters*) no ! tis the cadi—how disagreeable ! (*aside*)

Ben. Beautiful Zoe ! my gem of Golconda ! my gold-dust of the Ganges ! all the sweet salutations of the afternoon betide you !

Zoe. Your worship is very polite ; but indeed I wish you would not call at our cabin so frequently, when my husband is abroad.

Ben. Wherefore so, my nutmeg in blossom !

Zoe. Because I have neighbors, who sometimes will employ their eyes and ears.

Ben. Ay ! and their tongues afterwards, I suppose ; the scandalous wretches : ah ! Zoe ! this is a wicked world, and full of naughty talkers ; but there's a necessity for my visits : you know, I have private dealings with Alexis.

Zoe. But not with his wife.

Ben. Poh ! poh ! Alexis is a greek christian, who lives by the smuggling of forbidden liquors, and unless I were to stand his friend, he would be ruined : for the sale of wine among true believers, is contrary to the law of the land.

Zoe. And the *toleration* of it, contrary to the oath of your worship's office.

Ben. Hem ! my oath—why that is—hem ! something sticks in my throat. No, Zoe, no—you have formed quite a wrong opinion upon this subject ; I must expound to you : you dont understand law.

Zoe. No ; I simply pretend to common sense.

Ben. Now, I'll illustrate : tis true Alexis sells the wine, but then he sells it *privately ;* mark that, *privately :* and I, as the cadi, in mere consideration of—

Zoe. Just two thirds of the profit upon each flask—

Ben. Pshaw ! never mind the consideration :—as I was saying—Alexis sells the wine privately, and I also privately sell him——

Zoe. Your worship's sanction.

Ben. O, fy ! Zoe ; that's a vastly improper word :' a magistrate must never *sanction* a breach of the law : no, I sell him my—*ignorance.*

Zoe. How very rich your worship must be ! sure such a stock in trade can never be exhausted !

Ben. Ah, banterer ! well, now having explained the commercial arrangement between us, you must not chide me for this visit. Husband and wife, you know, are *one ;* and surely Zoe, his partner for life, I may be allowed to regard also as his partner in trade.

Zoe. If you please; but only as his *sleeping partner.*

Ben. Heigho ! Alexis is a happy man ! Zoe, dont you perceive something peculiar in the expression of these eyes ?

Zoe. Let me look : yes, they twinkle frightfully.

Ben. Ah ! that's a sentimental languor, Zoe ! I have a secret sorrow, you shall be my confidant ; I am distractedly in love with the most beautiful of her sex.

Zoe. True ; your worship has a wife : the lady Grumnildra.

Ben. Dont mention her, I beseech ; that nauseous old woman ! she is more terrible than the monsoons ; excepting that tygress Grimnigra, the wife of Mustapha, the emir, she is the most pestilent shrew in all Bagdat. No, Zoe, the object of *my* passion is a different creature. (*approaching*) She is now not very distant from me——

Zoe. (*retreating*) I wander still further in my doubts.

Ben I heave ! I throb ! I burn ! I blaze ! oh, Zoe ! behold your adorer at your feet ! (*he casts himself fantastically before her—she surveys him for a moment attentively, then bursts into a fit of immoderate laughter)*

Ben. Thou pitiless hyæna! dost thou deride my agonies.

Zoe. Ha, ha, ha! stay—dont get up yet, pray let me look at you a little longer—ha, ha, ha! (*Alexis looks in at the casement—Zoe gives a sudden sign and he checks himself)*

Ben. Does this prostration of thy victim gratify thee?

Zoe. O! yes, amazingly; kneel, I charge you, kneel.

Ben. I do, I do; now then murmur the soft confession in my ear—even as the nightingale woos the rose!

Zoe. Hold! if the fortress must capitulate; let me at least secure terms for the garrison! (ALEXIS *softly opens the door behind Benmoussaff, and holds it a-jar)*

TRIO—ZOE, BENMOUSSAFF, ALEXIS.

Zoe.	Mighty man! if I surrender,
	Pledge me first a solemn vow;
	Swear! to love with heart as tender
	Ever fierce and fond as now,
Ben.	I swear! ever! o! ever!
Zoe.	Mighty man! though rivals languish,
	Swear your love shall never stray—
	Ah, fond heart! that doubt is anguish—
	Swear! and make it easy, pray!
Ben.	I swear! never! o, never!
Zoe. (allegro)	Rise, and by my smiles rewarded
	Live by love supremely blest!
Ben.	By those radiant eyes regarded,
	Joys too vast invade my breast.
Alex. (*aside*)	Soon I'll change those sportive glances
	Into looks of graver sort.
Zoe.	Come, knit hands, I'll teach you dances;
	Swains are brisk who come to court.

Ben.   Though unskill'd in such advances
            I'll not baulk a lady's sport.
All.   Fal lal lal ! and lara, lara !
            Fal lal, &c.

(Zoe engages the cadi in a quick dance—Alexis steals forward by her signals and chassees into the figure—Benmoussaff attempts to stop, but they twirl him alternately from one to the other, and force him to continue till he reels with giddiness)

Alex. Ha, ha ! I crave permission to compliment your worship, upon the gracefulness of your motions ; I have seldom seen a dance sustained with so fanciful a spirit.

Ben. Bless me ! I'm quite out of breath ; why, I confess, Alexis, you have found me in rather a whimsical situation ; but I protest nothing immoral was intended :—I was merely persuading Zoe to practise a new step.

Alex. I'm afraid it was a *false* step ; at least, your worship must allow, that from the moment I became a spectator. you mistook your *time.*

Ben. He, he ! that's a pleasant jest ; you are a jocular fellow.

Alex Vastly jocular ; I'll make bold to give your worship a proof—*(tweaks him by the nose)* that's another pleasant jest !

Ben. Ah, ah ! here's an atrocious assault ; why, sirrah ! have you no respect for authority ?

Alex. Not when it is vested in hands that would abuse it.

Ben. Mighty fine ! is this your gratitude for my generous protection ?

Alex. An empty flask for your protection ! I have always bought it of you at double its value. Look ye, old whiskers ! you have lived half a century by extortion and rascality ; your very name is a polecat that infects the common air of Bagdat. Rich rogues have sometimes favors to sell, which honest poverty is compelled to purchase ; but the danger, as well as the offence is mutual ; and depend upon it if you threaten, the punishment also shall be equally divided.

Ben. Say you so—(*aside*) this fellow must be taken care of. Well, Alexis, I've a sweet temper, and dont take offence. Have you any more remarks to offer ?

Alex. Only one, it is this ; yonder stands the door—in the opposite corner is deposed a cudgel. Now, destiny sternly decrees, that either your worship's leg should chassee through the one, or the arm of your humble servant flourish the other : do I make myself understood ?

Ben. Perfectly ; the text is so obvious. I won't trouble you for an illustration. But hold ! before I depart let me warn you, in the name of the caliph, not to admit any stranger beneath this roof after sunset.

Alex. You may trust me—I have no partiality for intruders. (*jogging him towards the door*)

Ben. Well, well, dont hurry me : let me pass forth into the street with all the decorus dignity of a magistrate. I am now going to the bezestein, to recite the the caliph's proclamation to the citizens.

Alex. I and my camel shall attend the oration.

Ben. (*aside*) I shall be prepared for your reception. With your camel? how many flasks ? eh ?

Alex. I'll show my accounts in due time ; there's the door.

Ben. Dont hurry me, remember my dignity ; an official person like me——

Alex. Should take a hint—never remain in a place, till the stronger party is forced to turn him out. (*pushes him through the door into the street.*

Zoe. Ha ! ha ! Alexis ! applaud your Zoe for an excellent actress. Did I not cajole the ancient sinner dextrously ?

Alex. No angler e'er managed his bait with a prettier temptation. That iniquity upon crutches ! tis lucky for him I returned so soon, for had he wronged me of a single kiss, I'd have pounded his carcass to a mummy.

Zoe. No : believe me, I guarded my lips with a constancy worthy of our greek ancestors.

Alex. (*kissing her*) Ah! though noon be past, I feel morning's clearest dew yet clinging to these roses! I shall banquet greedily upon their sweets anon. (*going*)

Zoe. But whither now? nay, Alexis, is this well? abroad all day, yet quit me again so suddenly.

Alex. I left my camel in a neighbor's stall. I will but drive him once through the bezestein, just for the chance of a sly customer to an odd flask. Money, Zoe—ah! money must be made while we are young, or I and my camel shall pad the desert in our old age.

Zoe. Well, go thy ways—against thy return, I'll dress up our little board as daintily as loving housewife can provide.

Alex. Ay, wench, then for our supper and a flask of the old vintage.

Zoe. Then for a merry ballad and a tale of other times.

Alex. Till the wasted lamp flickers in its socket.

Zoe. As we sink to rest, memory in murmurs will bless heaven for the day that is past.

Alex. And in our dreams hope and fancy, like good-tempered fairies, will prattle of to-morrow.

DUET—ALEXIS—ZOE.

How boon are the hours after set of the sun,
When nature unzones and all labors are done :
The camel in gladness is led to his stall,
The distaff and spindle are hung by the wall ;
The lattices close, and our table is spread,
Poor greeks, it is true, on no dainties are fed,
But light are our spirits, as lightly we sup,
And the name of some relative sweetens each cup.

Proud mussulmen slumber on pillows of state—
Poor greeks sleep on rushes, yet blessing their fate :
The indolent rich seek but find not repose,
While industry's eye lids unconsciously close.
Red morning light strikes unreproved on our eyes,
For though to fresh labors it bids us arise,
Yet boon are the hours after set of the sun,
When nature unzones and all labors are done.

[*exeunt*

SCENE III—*the bezestein, crowded with characters of all descriptions.*

CHORUS.

O! now the bezestein is merry!
    With merchandize crying,
    With customers buying,
    With folk in all stations,
    With goods from all nations—
    Here business and pleasure,
    Make labor—take leisure—
    Dispersed yet united,
    And all well delighted—
For o! the bezestein is merry!

BENMOUSSAFF, *attended by his officers, comes forward, and collects the populace around him.*

CHANT—BENMOUSSAFF.

Good people of Bagdat! I charge you draw near,
And the law of the caliph with reverence hear!
This eve, after sun-set, no creature must roam,
But each loyal citizen speed to his home.
Your household's be muster'd, your lattices block'd,
And your gates against strangers religiously lock'd:
Whoever the streets in the dark hour shall tread,
For the fault of his *foot* shall atone with his *head*.
Good people, beware! ere the night watches come,
Your signal will strike on the evening drum.

(*people to each other*)

Ah, neighbor, beware! ere the night-watches come!
Your signal will strike on the evening drum.

ALEXIS *enters, leading his camel laden with panniers.*

Sand o! sand from the desert!
    Who'll buy my sand?
            C

CHORUS.

O! now the bezestein is merry! &c.

(during the repeat of the chorus, Alexis appears, selling small bags from the right hand pannier—Benmoussaff observes, and taking aside an ancient female, seems to counsel her in dumb show)

Old W. (approaching Alexis) Friend! I would be your customer for a bag of this same sand : truly, the fame of it is mightily noised in Bagdat.

Alex. (aside) Now, this must be a jolly old toper, by the devoutness of her aspect. My noble lady, let me serve you.

Old W. Hold, friend! methinks I snuff a delicious odor from the *opposite* pannier—is there a difference in your sand?

Alex. (aside) Yes—the fume of the flask has stung her delicate nose already. Hem! the bags in this pannier contain some curious sand of a moister quality.

Old W. I'll deal with you for a sample. Will this sequin purchase me a bag?

Alex. Your ladyship is liberal. *(delivers a large bag, aside to her)* If, when you reach home, any thing extraordinary should be found in the bag——

Old W. Nay, I'll not defer an examination so long —luckily the cadi is at hand to assist me. Neighbors, I pray you, behold the contents of my purchase. *(produces the flask)* Ah! I shall faint—the irreligious wretch has sold me wine!

Alex. (moves away) Sand o! who'll by my sand?

Ben. (rushing forward) Stop him there! seize upon that knave and his camel!

Alex. Eh! how! seize my camel! master Benmoussaff? what's the meaning of this?

Ben. I shall explain that presently. Search that left-hand pannier!

Alex. Holloa! search my panniers! why, master Benmoussaff——

Ben. Observe! he winks his eyes at me—but I dont understand him.

Officer. (*searching*) The pannier is full, and every bag contains a flask.

Ben. O the impiety of the times! my feelings are quite shocked! thou naughty infidel! I here confiscate thy camel with its burden, and command thee to pay down upon the spot, the lawful fine of fifty sequins, or forthwith be lodged within the prison.

Alex. Oho! I smell the roguery now. Good people —neighbors—friends! listen while I expose this perjured old caitiff, and——

Ben. Stop his mouth! he is going to revile the caliph, and that's high treason.

Alex. No, villain—tis his infamous officer.

Ben. That's petty treason. Stop his mouth, I say!

Officer. (*uncorks a flask*) Marry! by its smell, this should be old wine of the finest flavor.

Ben. Old wine! say you? that aggravates the wickedness.

Old W. Good master cadi! I pray you let a pile presently be kindled in the centre of the bezestein, and the accursed liquor, publicly consumed.

Ben. Not publicly—that would give too much importance to the affair—no—carry the liquor to my house, and I'll take care it shall be consumed in *private.*

Alex. Ah! robber! marauder! cut purse!

Ben. Ah! protect me, good people! if you love justice, and reverence virtue—I give my person into your hands as a sacred deposit.

Alex. (*straggling*) Rage! vengeance! devils!

Ben. Do you hear him? there's impiety! drag the infidel to prison!

MUSICAL COLLOQUY.

Ben. Away to the prison! guards drag him away!
Alex. For a cudgel to pound thee to powder I pray!
Guards. Away!
Alex. Fire and furies!
Ben. Oh! hear how he swears!
All. The law is regardless of threats or of prayers!

zoe enters and rushes to her husband.

Zoe.   Ah! whither, Alexis, my life art thou borne?
Alex.   From love and from Zoe by baseness I'm torn.
Zoe.   Kind neighbors! behold with compassion my
                        wo!
Alex.   O! loosen my arms!
B..n.   I shall catch my death blow!
All.   The tumult increases—she pleads and he
                        swears——
            But law is regardless of threats or of pray-
                        ers!

(*the evening drum beats, instantaneously the crowd
disperses—Alexis submits to his fate, and Zoe overwhelmed by despair, retires upon the opposite side—
as the populace separate they murmur to each other*)

            Ah! neighbor, beware lest the night watches
                        come,
            Our signal *now* strikes on the evening drum.

———————————————

SCENE IV—*a street in Bagdat—the evening drum
beats without—citizens cross, retiring to their houses—they enter their respective doors—presently after the lattices are closed before the windows, and a
general stillness prevails—as the music dies away,*
ALMANZOR *enters with a slow and measured step,
supporting* ORASMYN.

Alm. Onward! nay, onward! sweetest boy!
Oras. I cannot uncle! in sooth I cannot—my limbs
faint under me, and all their strength is gone.
Alm. Yet bear up but a little, and we reach our
friends.
Oras. Ah, me! where are they, uncle! sure, we
have journeyed far to seek them; this is our fifth long
day of pilgrimage. Yesternight, you said that we had
gai..ed the desert's edge, and there our camels founder-
ed. I slept beneath a palm tree's pleasant shade and my
dreams were happy; but you scared them suddenly

102

and long ere dawn, while yet the east was dark, still
" onward !" was your cry. O ! we have thrided for-
ests, climbed rocks, and forded floods, through all the
burning hours of noon, to reach this vast strange place.
Nay, I shall find my grave before my friends if we
must travel further.

Alm. Courage, Orasmyn ! our journey is accomplish-
ed. Thou standest now in Bagdat : even in that great
proud city of whose wonders oft times by the watch-
fire's blaze, at nights I have discoursed to thee.

Oras. I little prize such wonders ; they please not
like the simple home that we have quitted. Oh ! at
this hour, this sun-set hour, methinks there was a soft
and solemn charm that brooded ever o'er our desert
dwelling ; would that I now might hear the curtains of
our tent idly flapping to the breeze ; or mark the peli-
can on homeward wing, bearing the far drawn waters
to her thirsty brood ! ah ! scenes beloved and lost !
uncle ! my tears start freshly at each dear remembrance.

Alm. Cheer thee, my gentle boy ! hence with these
sickly musings ; the brilliant star of thy nativity directs
our course. Enterprize invites, and fortune twines thee
with a favoring arm ! come lean on this staff, and onward !

Oras. I cannot, uncle ! in truth I cannot : nay, let
me rest awhile against this bulk ; my forehead fevers
and my lips grow parched : ah ! that I might drink.

Alm. (aside) What measure may I best pursue,
The burying-ground lies yet far distant : that sacred
solitude once gained, we might in safety rest till the
appointed hour ; but ah ! those tender limbs ! without
refreshment they deny their office. Here stands a car-
avansary ! its gates thus early closed ! methinks, fifteen
divorcing years have strangely altered Bagdat since I
knew it last. I can remember well this street, a crowded thorough-fare ; and now, a death-like stillness hangs
upon each threshold : the change is well ; its present
privacy is mated to my wish. I'll strike against the
gate and ask admittance. (*Almanzor beat. . the gate,*

C 2

an interval elapses—he stri es again—a lattice opens above, and a citizen looks forth)

Cit. What daring hand is thine, to strike against my gate at this forbidden hour? speak, what are you?

Alm. Weary way farers, who claim that common hospitality to which your sign inviteth all who travel.

Cit. Begone! begone! ye luckless wanderers! know ye not the caliph's law? 'tis death to be abroad in Bagdat, now the sun hath set! *(music at distance)* hark! the guard approaches—begone, if ye love safety—I dare not hold a longer parley. *(closes the lattice)*

Alm. (as paralysed by sudden fears) Mysterious heavens! are we then betrayed? can the usurper yet suspect——

Oras. (running to him) Uncle! the blood forsakes your cheek, and sure you tremble——

Alm. Tis for thee, dear boy! for thee!

Oras. Nay, sir! where's my danger?

Alm. Hush! hush! the guards are close—this way! no—no—by all directions they advance at once.

(music becomes loud and louder—guards enter upon all sides—the strangers endeavor to escape in vain—they are surrounded—GIAFAR enters—music ceases)

Giaf. Who, and what are you, that transgress the law? 'tis Giafar, Alraschid's vizier, who demands your rank.

Alm. Dread sir! our ignorance, and not our will offends. We are strangers from the arabian desert, who but entered Bagdat by the western gate, even as day forsook this world.

Giaf. Whither tends your journey?

Alm. Far as the distant Tartary. We would visit the great fair at Samarcande.

Giaf. Have ye relatives or friends in Bagdat?

Alm. (after a short pause) Alas! poor wandering arabs boast no social ties with polished man; our deserts and our liberty are all our birth right.

Giaf. What youth is he, who trembles and averts his face?

Alm. Poor way-worn child ! an orphan, sir, confi-
ded to my charge.

Giaf. Let me behold him closer—come hither, boy !

Oras. You will not harm me, sir ! indeed, I never
injured *you*——

Giaf. Fear not, my innocent ! (*Giafar gazes scru-
tinizingly in Orasmyn's face—Almanzor watches in
alarm*) *my doubts are satisfied.* Strangers ! ye both
are free ; at yonder guard house seek refreshment ;
rove afterwards through Bagdat as ye list—some open
porch will yield a licensed shelter for the night.

Alm. The wanderers benizon, rest with you, sir. (*he
catches Orasmyn's hand*) Come, boy ! come ! (*music
of march—Giafar waves his hand—the strangers bow
low, and pass—guards follow, Aladin and Nourreddin remain with Giafar*)

Giaf. By allah ! they are found. Age, feature,
garb, all, *all* conspire in proof ! Aladin ! hie to the palace and present this ring ! Alraschid will divine its im-
port. [*exit Aladin*] Nourreddin ! say, after the rack
had forced his secret, where didst thou lodge the arab
slave ?

Nour. Deep in a cell, under the seraglio garden.

Giaf. Blessed be that chance. which cast the traitor
in my power, and dragged this dark conspiracy to light.
The caliph hath himself adventured, alas too daringly
I doubt, to pierce the traitor's haunt and prove deci-
sively Cephania's faith. Two hours hence rejoin me
at the tomb of Ali, till then your watch is known : this
night is laboring with a wild event and, if we prosper,
Alraschid's sacred throne, stands fixed for ever !

[*exeunt separately*

SCENE V—*an ancient burying ground, planted with cypresses. over which are scattered monuments in ruin
—the horizon is now entirely dark—it thunders at
a distance—*ALMANZOR *leads forward* ORASMYN
from among the tombs.

Alm. Hail ! reverend earth ! to each of thine eternal thresholds hail! *(he casts himself upon one of the forward ruins, and points towards another for Orasmyn)* Rest thee, Orasmyn! the wished-for goal is reached, and here our travel ends.

Oras. Here! in this desolate, bewildered place! where at each foot-fall the hollow ground returns an hundred echoes! you told me we should lodge with gentle friends ; and none but savage spirits should inhabit here   Sure you do but jest !

Alm. Regard my speech as holiest truth.   Rejoice, thou weary one! for *here* is rest.

Oras. No, no ; way-worn as I am, I would freshly task these tottering limbs till they sank under me rather than make my pillow in so loathed a den.   Dear uncle, let us hence! the night is troublous and portends a storm.   Nay, hark ye there! already the thunder rolls at distance! this ground shakes under me, and yon tall cypresses so moan and mutter in the rising gust, that now a chilly sickness creeps about my heart.

Alm. Fear not, Orasmyn! thou art with the *dead*! the passive, peaceful, uninjurious *dead*! *(he rises, and points with his staff majestically around)*—Boy! these broken monuments and ruined graves, from whose blest touch thy shivering spirit now recoils, are chambers of the brave, and wise, and good! heroes, sages, bards, imperishable men! whose forms have been in elder time, whose deeds are now, and shall be ages hence. Glory's rich heirs! memory's beloved wards! *here*, in a long sweet sleep of blessedness they wait the summons of eternal love! boy! regard yon shadowy pile, that lifts its sculptured sorrows loftier than the rest!

Oras. That, where the marble most is fractured?

Alm. Ay, boy! gaze, reverently gaze! within that mouldering sepulchre, the noblest, best, most honored of this earth reposes.   Boy, unconscious boy! there sleeps—*thy father* !

Oras. My father! said you? *(he springs towards the tomb, and falls against its front)* oh, let me kneel before its hallowed bound; thus pour my tears and kisses on these cold damp bars that intercept my passage,

here cling and fix for ever :—a living statue, wa ch-
ful to protect my parent's dust!

Alm. My child! forbear these transports; nay, I
command thee rise!

Oras. Alas! for pity.   Say, sir. how fell my father?

Alm. Mournfully, yet with a hero's constant pride.
Within his palace walls, beset by multitudes, pierced
with innumerous wounds, and still to life's last gasp
defending and defying! so fell Almanzor's brother : so
Orasmyn's sire!

Oras. Who was the impious cause of such a deed?

Alm. Even the sire of him who now holds sway in
Bagdat, and with the father's throne inherits still the father's hate: of him who now detains our lost Cephania in disgraceful bonds, and lives to prove thy dead-
liest foe and mine.

Oras. His name?

Alm. (*with bitter emphasis*) Haroun Alraschid!

Oras. Haroun Alraschid? nay, I remember well,
while yet an infant, when first I raised my little hands
in prayer, you then pronounced that name with fearful
force and bade me curse it.

Alm. (*kindling into fury*) Ay! that did I, boy! as
from thy childhood, so to thy latest age preserve that
curse. Come, clinch thy hand with mine, and I will
teach thee direr forms of malediction. Tremendous
genii! ye who watch by night, attentive though unseen ; spirits of air. or fire, or grosser earth—to you
aloud I first renew those ancient words of hate.—
Cursed be the son of Ali's murderer ! cursed be Haroun Alraschid! yea, cursed! cursed!

(*the hurricane suddenly bursts forth—the thunder
rolls tremendously, and lightnings glare between
the tombs and cypresses—an ÆTHIOP, wildly habited, who has apparently lain slumbering upon a
fragment of the middle sepulchre, leaps up from his
posture to the summit of the ruin, and extends his
right arm in adjuration to the clouds—the lightning's flash displays his figure*)

Æth. (*aloud*) Cursed be the name Almanzor curs-
eth! yea, cursed be Haroun Alraschid!

Alm. (*after a pause of trepidation*) What wild fantastic shape art thou, that in this stormy hour and
place of graves thus strangely dost encounter both our
steps and words?—pronounce, uncertain thing, what
may'st thou be?

Æth. (*springing from the ruin*) One of the earth,
yet scorning that I tread!—the stars forewarned me
of this wished event, and bade me offer homage to my
chosen lords. (*he prostrates himself*) Hail to thee,
arabian sage! hail, thrice hail, to thee, child of the
desert!

Alm. Thy purpose then is friendly?

Æth. Else this swift arm had whirled this gleaming
javelin to thy heart.

Oras. Nay, dearest uncle, trust him not!—tis sure
some spirit; let us fly!

Alm. Hush thee, boy. (*advancing to the Æthiop
with a hesitating confidence*) If thou art rightly friend,
answer these words. Medina's hopeful birth ?

Æth. (*grasps his hand, and replies with solemnity*) Mecca's fulfilling tomb!

Alm. Enough! at once I clasp thee to my heart, assured!—thou then art he appointed as our guide?

Æth. What other should I seem? come, let the
wild adventure of our course begin.

Alm. Have with thee! (*points mysteriously to the
sepulchre*) which is the fragment we must first re-
move?

Æth. The corner marble of the topmost step;—
through the dark vast beyond, this horn must then be
sounded thrice. Come.

Alm. Soft! a moment: lest his childish spirit falter
at such scenes, first let me bind Orasmyn's eyes. Boy,
kneel down before me.—Now, lend thy handkerchief.

Oras. Ah me! what mean you, sir?

Alm. Obey! and whatsoe'er betides, still keep thou
silent.

(Almanzor fixes the bandage—the boy clasps his hands together, and remains kneeling in mute prayer—the Æthiop approaches the sepulchre—he removes the marble, stoops and applies his horn to the cavity, it sounds thrice—the tempest rages around with deafening violence—the sepulchre slowly yawns asunder, and discloses a dark and frightful chasm—as the thunder ceases, a chant of subterranean voices is heard to rise)

SUBTERRANEAN CHORUS.

Welcome! welcome! mortal feet,
Now the quick and dead shall meet—
From the land, and from the waves—
Welcome! all who covet graves!

(a thin quivering flame now springs up, and flickers about the edge of the chasm—Almanzor and the Æthiop each seize upon a hand of the kneeling boy, and forcibly lead him to the brink of the chasm)

Oras. (struggling) Hold! hold! *(by a sudden effort he tears away the bandage from his eyes)* ah! whither have ye drawn me? what gulf is this?—mercy, mercy! fires gleam, and ghastly figures glide below! ah, save me, save me! *(he clings in agony about Almanzor's robe)*

Alm. (repulsing him, and stamping his foot imperatively) Descend!

Æth. (planting his javelin against his breast) This instant! or I strike!

Oras. Allah! guard thy servant!

(the terrified boy, exhausted by his struggles, sinks despairingly at Almanzor's feet—the subterranean chant is renewed, while the storm, with redoubled fury, revisits the scene above—Almanzor with the Æthiop, support the boy between them, and descend the gulf as the curtain falls)

END OF THE FIRST ACT.

ACT II.

SCENE I.—*interior of a vast catacomb, lighted at intervals by funeral lamps—on one side shields and weapons piled together in the shape of a rude altar —on the other side a pillar with an engine at its base appears to sustain a portion of the roof—*ORASMYN *is discovered upon the step of the altar, supported between* ALMANZOR *and the* ÆTHIOP—*conspirators of the race of Ali, encircle him in adoration.*

CHORUS.

Child of the desert ! awful rise
As the red moon through vaporish skies !
Child of the desert ! glorious beam
As the fresh sun on indian stream.

Oras. Ye unknown dwellers of the secret earth ! who bow before me and thus hem me round—say, why this homage ? how have I deserved these songs of praise ? you look as if you meant me kindly—but sure your postures and your words are mockery.

1st Consp. Hail ! eastern star !

2d Consp. Hail ! ruler over mighty nations !

3d Consp. (*a priest*) Hail ! our prophet's emblem upon earth !

Oras. Peace, peace ! my heart will break, if I am taunted thus !

Alm. Child of my care ! let not amazement, like a frost, benumb thy spirit, and suddenly my speech shall change these wonders to a stedfast joy. O'er these, and me, and all, reign prince for ever ! for thou art rightfully proud Bagdat's lord ! —fifteen years since, in his unguarded hour, the royal Ali lost both throne and life : I saw my brother fall—his palace blaze ! my only niece, some few years elder than thy little self, was borne to slavery. Thou, Orasmyn ! of all this dear, lamented wreck, thou only wert preserved. I bore thee

closely nestled twixt my shield and breast, through all
opposing dangers of the night ; and reached by miracle
a sheltering bourne.   Safe to the desert's burning depth
I fled, and far from man, man's future ruler reared,
yea ! reared him worthily for empire and revenge!

CHORUS.

Hail ! son of Ali ! hail ! thrice hail !

Alm. Behold, in this confederated band, thy natural friends, the relics of thy race.   Here, while the
cheated foe believed thee dead, in this prodigious char-
nel stored with arms, from year to year, these patriots
have convened, commemorating still thy birth with
hymns, and sagely scheming to redeem thy rights.   The
time appointed by thy natal star, for glorious enterprize, now crowns their watch ! greet them, Orasmyn !
with endearing words ; such as may suit a sovereign's
lips, their love, their constancy, and this auspicious
hour !

Oras. Amazed with doubts, made giddy while I trust,
I wish to thank them, yet despair of means.   Kind
men ! you loved my father, fought round him when he
fell ; I find no words to pay your service, but feel that
I could die to satisfy such friends ! speak for me, sir !
declare my duties, say, what must I do ?

Alm. Avenge thy murdered sire—thy suffering race !

Oras. How ? how ?

Alm. (*solemnly lifting a dagger deposited on the altar*) Grasp this tremendous poniard ! round whose blade
thy father's life-drops cling in crimson rust, swear !
ne'er to rest till thou hast sheathed this steel deep in
the heart of his destroyer's son ; till Bagdat dreadfully
atone her crime ; till massacre and havoc choke her
streets ; her turrets fall ; her palaces consume ; and
vengeance stalk sole monarch o'er the scene !

Oras. O ! horror ! horror !

Æth. (*vehemently grasping his hand*) Ay ! blood !
a sea of blood ! then fires as red, to sport and sparkle
on its boiling waves.   Hail ! beauteous carnage ! hail !

D

thrice lovely flames ! prononce the glorious covenant !
swear, prince, swear !

Oras. Away ! must I win sceptres with a murderer's hand ? climb to a throne o'er mangled carcasses,
and hear my reign proclaimed by howling matrons and
the orphan's cry ? never ! for others keep your fatal
greatness and the pomp that damns. Leave me to
deserts and my first obscurity ; but with me leave my
careless innocence and unreproaching heart !

Alm. Eternal allah ! live I to this shame ? is this
an Ali ? this my brother's son ? thou soft, degenerate : yet hold my rage ! boy ! if one natural drop yet
warm thy veins, one pulse beat faithful to its god-like
spring, as thou would'st shun my hate, my mortal curse,
be sudden to convince me of thy birth, lest I write
strumpet on thy mother's grave ; rend with these ancient hands that fraudful form, and strew thy limbs in
madness round these vaults !

Oras. Merciful heavens ! to what am I devoted !

Alm. To fame and glory, or a coward's grave ! pro-
voke me longer, and this arm ! but no, thou wilt not
break the old fond heart that loves thee.

Oras. Ah ! weeping ! tears in such reverend eyes !
nay, then indeed I'm lost ! (*he takes the poniard with
trembling hand*) come ! dreadful record ! ah ! said
you my father's blood ?

Alm. Swear to avenge it ! swear it ! swear it !

Æth. By heaven and hell ! attesting angels and a-
venging dæmons swear !

Oras. I swear ! ghost of my father ! hear thy wretched son, and—ah ! I grow dizzy—clouds—dark—dark !
(*he drops insensible upon the earth*)

Alm. Orasmyn ! speak ! look up, I charge thee : nay,
he is cold !—my boy ! my boy !

3d Consp. He swoons ! the harrassed mind and body could sustain no more ; nay, gently bear him to the
cell within, there kindly cordials shall renew the life.

Æth. The prince hath sworn ! remember ye ! tis
sworn !

*(some bear Orasmyn in, while the priest re-deposits the
poniard on the altar, and scatters incense from a
censer)*

CHORUS.

Rest! ghost of Ali! rest in peace!

Alm. Now my confederates! to our great resolve!
When bursts the lightning! who directs the flash?
How falls the tyrant? speak! our course? our means!
    3d Consp. The temper of the people now is apt—
Since first the trusty slave announced thy coming;
Our friends with prophecy and omens strange,
Have hourly practised on the vulgar mind——
Amidst the mosques, nay, in Alraschid's court,
Our vast conspiracy hath secret springs.
This morn, Abudah of the palace guard,
Publish'd our summons on the centry's walk.
Meantime, by tapestry near the shrine conceal'd,
I scared the kneeling priests with words like heaven's!
Doubts, fears, and scruples shake the general heart:
Now sudden deeds were best.   To-morrow's eve—
    Æth. To morrow! why delay the glorious blow?
This night, this very hour, assail the palace,
Devote Alraschid midst his slumbering guards,
And yield all Bagdat to avenging fires!
    Priest. (aside to Almanzor) I like this noble passion
                in your friend,
His flashing eyes declare no common soul,
What is his name? his rank?
    Alm. Why question *me* ?
Who till this hour ne'er gazed upon his form.
    Priest. Has he not been the comrade of your road?
    Alm. But now, among the tombs, we first encoun-
                ter'd,
He was appointed to conduct us hither.
    Priest. No ; Caled, your arabian slave, who bore
This morn your letter to Cephania,
He was directed from the sun-set hour
To watch above, and guide you down these shades.

113

Alm. Is not this Æthiop known among our band?
Abudah! Hassan!

(*the conspirators gather round Almanzor, who appears to question them—their eyes are then directed towards the Æthiop with disquiet—he watches their gestures and suddenly obtrudes upon their circle*)

Æth. By your leave, grave friends!
Admit me one in this divan of whisperers;
Come! I've a quick sure eye to read mens' hearts;
I am your topic, what would you inquire?
I'st who and what I am?—I answer thus,
I was a stranger; *now* I know you all.
My skin is of night's own color; for my heart—
'Tis sure a bold one, since I've ventured here:
Perchance an honest one, that's as you use me!

Alm. Audacious ruffian! darest thou to betray?

Æth. Forbear, thou snow crown'd Ætna cramm'd
          with fires!
Forbear! thou rash old man; first hear, then chide;
Alraschid is thy foe, so is he mine:
Deep, deadly, lasting as my life, the hate
I bear him.   Ali's blood I may not boast,
Yet Ali's quarrel would I serve; stretch forth
Your arms, if ye are wise, and clasp a friend!

Alm. By what close treason did'st thou first acquire
A knowledge of our plans and guidance hither?

Æth. A super human power inform'd my soul,
Man is my master, yet I govern spirits!
'Tis written in fate's book, an Ali's hand
Alone must smite the tyrant; else years past
This hand had dealt the blow.   Oh! I have wasted
Whole nights o'er caldrons, communing with fiends,
To shape fit horrors for this destined hour.
Behold this wand of ebony! tis carved
With spells: myself, and all I touch, its power
Can render viewless.   Save to such clear'd eyes
As Mahomet blesses! bind me to your cause,
And presently I'll lead you to your prey,
All like thin air, through hosts of watchful guards
Invisible and safe! how say you, sirs?

114

Alm. I will not scorn thee, till I've proved thee
    false:
Thou say'st, that wand can render thee at will
Unseen though present. *Now,* perform the feat!
  Æth. (*after a pause*) Thou did'st mistake my
    speech; tis true I said,
And true I'll vouch that say, my art can cast
Illusion o'er all eyes the prophet loves n.:
But Ali's children are his dearest .u
I may not practise on the blest with spells?
  Alm. Nor shalt thou with thy words, detected
    cheat!
Mark! how a plain truth dashes these liars!
If thou rulest spirits, bid them save thee now!
(*Almanzor draws his poniard—the other conspirators*
  follow his example—the Æthiop retreats against the
  altar, and brandishing his javelin keeps them at
  bay)
  Æth. Hold! frantic and ungrateful that ye are!
Nay, if I needs must die, come on! I'll send
Some twenty ghosts before me on my road!
  Voice from above. Ho! there!
  Alm. Who call'd?
  Priest. Tis Almoran, our watch.

      ALMORAN *appears upon the roof.*

  Alm. Danger's abroad! strange steps and countless
    torches
Move o'er our heads! tis sure the caliph's guard!
  Priest. (*to Almanzor*) Dismiss all fear;—here we
    might mock whole armies;
Yon pillar holds immoveable and close
The ponderous stone before the sepulchre—
Till that's removed all human search were vain,
This engine at its base, alone can sink it.
  Æth. O! for an arm like fabled Hercules!
(*he darts with lightning speed across, seizes upon the*
  engine, and while the conspirators stand astounded
  at his action, he turns the wheel—the pillar instan-
  taneously sinks—the stone rolls away from the
        D 2

*mouth of the sepulchre, and the entrance from the
burial ground becomes visible)*

Æth. (triumphantly) Despair, bold spirits ! where's
your safety now ?

The storm is up ! the whelming waves drive on ;
Now trust me frankly, or partake my ruin !
Nay, nay, no idle ravings ! hold this lance ;
If I prove false, strike to my heart ; till then
Obey this wand !—we live or fall together !

*(he waves his arm commandingly—the conspirators
with involuntary obedience range in a line beyond
the altar—the Æthiop stands in front, projecting the
wand towards the middle of the stage—Almanzor
points the javelin to his heart—NOURREDDIN with
a torch, appears at the mouth of the sepulchre)*

RECITATIVE *accompanied.*

Nour. Who stirs below ? who thrids the gloom ?

ECHO *answers.*

Is't echo that replies ?
Or doth an answer rise
From startled sleepers of the tomb ?

GIAFAR *and guards with torches appear.*

Giaf. All hush'd !—Nourreddin ! lift thy torch and
lead
Before me to the search—the rest remain !

*(Nourreddin and Giafar descend the narrow winding
steps, and enter—they pause in the centre)*

Nay, not a form or sound ! the dead alone
Seem dwellers round us—flash the torch beyond !

*(Nourreddin strikes the light full upon the figures of
the conspirators—Giafar's eye wanders slowly over
the space they occupy, unconscious of their presence)*

Still all is solitude ! dim funeral lamps
But gleam on silent men whose flames are out
For ever ! doubtless the late hurricane,
Whose lightnings strew the ground above with ruins,
Hath split the marble threshold of this tomb.

Peace to its slumbering trust ! break we not longer
Mortality's dear sabbath ; pass and return !
(*Giafar and Nourreddin re ascend—they disappear*
with the guards from the opening—the sound of
their retreating steps rapidly dies away in distance
—the Æthiop retains his attitude unmoved—Al-
manzor drops the lifted javelin, and bends his eyes
abashed upon the ground—all the other conspirators,
sink involuntarily on their knees in awful homage
—the Æthiop slowly relaxes from his abstraction,
and haughtily surveys the group before he speaks)
　　Æth. How ! are the proud knees humbled ! cry you
　　　　　mercy !
This to a liar, a detected cheat !
(*to Almanzor*) Droops your crest also, wrathful sir ?
　　　　　I thought
That arm ere now, like his that rolls the thunder,
Had dealt out fate ; why falls the threatening lance ?
And wherefore hesitates arabian justice ?
　　Alm. What fellow man did ne'er achieve, is now
Thy boast ; thou hast subdued Almanzor ; seek
No prouder triumph. Whether heaven or hell
Be parent to thy art, I will not ask ;
Be ours at once, and name thine own reward.
　　Æth. Now you speak nobly, and our hands may
　　　　　meet !
Let thrones and treasures pay another's claim,
The kiss of beauty be the Æthiop's boon !
One word shall shape my vast reward—*Cephania !*
　　Alm. How said'st thou ?
　　Æth. Ay ! thy niece. The caliph's bride !
Now then the marvel's out : at once you spy
The jealous hate that weds me to your cause.
Alraschid's queen reigns lady of this soul.
Long years in secret have I sigh'd her slave.
Stern force hath bound the captive fair to one
She doubtless loathes, the curse of all her race.
Swear, when her thraldom ends, to yield her mine,
And boundless empire shall requite the gift !
　　Alm. By Ali's ghost, I swear !—Cephania's thine !

117

Speak, friends, what voices join with mine?

Con. All, all!

Æth. Enough! possess me presently with all your
    plan—

A written list of every secret friend—

And general knowledge of your means—thus once

Inform'd, I'll lead you to insured success

Bring forth the prince; to counsel, then to arms!

Alm. For great revenge!

Æth. For *love,* far greater!

Alm. Orasmyn's throne!

Æth. Cephania's bridal kiss!

CHORUS.

Solo.   Where are the scimetar's famous in story,
           That flash'd through the war-storm like
             meteors of glory?

Solo.   They rest and they rust on our forefather's
           graves.

Semi-Cho. Shall the sons of the mighty live dastards
           and slaves?

Full Cho. No!—by angel and fiend!—no—by earth,
           air, and fire!
           The son of an Ali is true to his sire!

*(they impetuously break the altar, and each conspira-
tor snatches up his arms, as it divides into pieces)*

           Each the steel and each the shield
           That his sire was wont to wield—
           Who shall conquer him who fights
           For his father's ravish'd rights?
           Tyrants! of the fray beware!
           Freedom and revenge are there!

*(Almanzor and the Æthiop bring forward Orasmyn,
and place again the poniard in his hand—the conspirators compose a pyramid with their shields, upon which they elevate his figure, and the scene closes
upon the group)*

SCENE II—*a hall in the house of Mustapha the emir.*

enter MUSTAPHA, *pursued by* GRIMNIGRA.

Grim. Wretch! traitor! libertine!

Must. Bleat not so troublously, my tender lamb!—gentlest Grimnigra, I prithee be pacified.

Grim. Pacified, quotha! I'll scream the knowledge of my wrongs round all Bagdat first ;—false, sensual traitor! have I not detected thee in the very fact of immorally soliciting one of my handmaids? thou base-spirited renegade! how could'st thou stoop from the dignified embraces of a Grimnigra, to court the vulgar caresses of her slave?

Must. Angel of purity! credit thy faithful spouse, when he declares——

Grim. Traitor! peace ;—thus I am rewarded for my condescension, when by an alliance with this hand I elevated thee from plebeian insignificance to the proud distinctions of an emir!—ah! wherefore did the great grand daughter of a sultan, the widow of a ba-shaw, and the first cousin of the mufti, so fatally forget the glories of her rank ?—but tremble, caitiff, the same hand that hath exalted can in turn depress ;—the muf-ti may redress my wrongs, and a single complaint to my cousin in the morning, secures to my husband a present of the bow-string in the afternoon.

Must (*aside*) That argument always chokes me.

Grim. O! my dear deceased husband! these are pious tears to thy memory! thou wert a virtuous man ; why I am destined to bewail thy early loss ?

Must. Early! why, the good man was ninety-six when he died, and without vanity I think that his suc-cessor——

Grim. Offer not the odious comparison, plebeian that thou art, wasn't my husband a bashaw with three tails ?

Must. He was a magnificent man, I confess ; but in point of affection, oh! Grimnigra! will no caress-es soften ? (*kisses her hand*)

Grim. O! susceptibility! thou bane of woman!

well; this once I extend my gracious pardon, but if ever again——

enter a SLAVE.

Slave. A young female requests admission to your lordship in private.

Grim. Ah! an assignation made under my very roof!

Slave. I think tis on some matters of the magistracy; she talks of ill-usage from the cadi Benmoussaff.

Grim. Oh! in that case indeed! you have my consent to admit her.

Must. Thanks to my angel for her complaisance—you know this Benmoussaff is an enemy of mine.

Grim. He treats his amiable wife, my friend Grumnildra, with flagrant neglect, therefore I abhor him. (*aside to slave*) Hark'ye! is this female handsome?

Slave. (*aside*) Too much so for a private interview. [*exit*

Grim. Hem! well, my Mustapha! I shall now leave you awhile to the duties of your office.

Must. One chaste embrace to seal my pardon!

Grim. Deluder! I am all thine own! but never forget, my beloved Mustapha! no, even in the midst of our tenderest endearments, I charge you never forget that your affectionate wife can order you to be strangled whenever she pleases! [*exit*

Must. What a tigress! but she's old, tremendously old; the dear deceased bashaw must soon have her again snug by his side, and then—eh! by Mahomet's whiskers! a most delicate creature!

enter ZOE, *who kneels to him.*

Zoe. Gracious emir!

Must. Rise, my fair suppliant and impart thy grievance.

Zoe. Oh! my lord! I come for justice on the wicked cadi, Benmoussaff; I am told your lordship's power is absolute in this quarter of the city.

Must. It is. Go on; you are a vastly well informe..
young woman.

Zoe. This wicked cadi, my lord, has cast my husband into prison upon a false pretence, purely out of
revenge, because I had repulsed his odious attempts upon my honor.

Must. Oh! the reprobate! so you have sought my
protection against his naughty schemes?

Zoe. Yes, my lord, and I humbly would solicit——

Must. Rather say command; those eyes, fair creature! have a power to—so you say this terrible cadi
wanted——

Zoe. Yes, my lord, he *wanted*—but thank heaven!
my virtue——

Must. Ay, virtue's a fine thing, a very fine thing, to
be talked of. But you acted wisely, child! a cadi to
presume : had he been an emir indeed——

Zoe. My lord!

Must. Hark'ye, child!—your husband, you say, is in
prison; profit by the present opportunity, and your fortune may be made for life.

Zoe. I dont comprehend you, my lord.

Must. In a word, bestow upon the emir those favors you have denied the cadi; and this weighty purse
of sequins—(*forces a purse into Zoe's hand, which
she indignantly dashes upon the ground*)

Zoe. Is trampled upon in scorn, as the representa-
tive of a villain!

Must. Here's a virago! is the girl a lunatic? dont
I offer you gold, and that can purchase——

Zoe. Every thing, but the peace of mind you would
tempt me to sell for it. Shame! shame! reflect, my
lord, was any daring libertine to assail the honor of
your own wife——

GRIMNIGRA *silently opens the door of the inner
room, and steals forward.*

Must. Would to heaven such a man could be found
—I'd buy up all the horses in Arabia for his use, that
he might carry off the old nuisance as far as the red sea!

Grim. (stepping forward) Say you so, traitor ?—your real sentiments are divulged at last.

Must Oh! Mahomet! I feel the bow-string about my throat already. *(aside)*

Grim. I suspected some licentious project, and quietly stole into the next apartment on purpose that I might confound the whole iniquity.—*(to Zoe)* Young woman! I applaud your correct principles : you repulsed the tempter with becoming dignity :—and as you are in distress, I am inclined, as a token of my esteem, to present you with——

Zoe. Oh, thanks! dear beneficent lady!

Grim. But no—on reflection, the gift of money would derogate from the merit of a good action, and virtue is its own reward. So, go thy ways, child, and instead of my purse I shall give you my prayers.

Zoe. Oh! world! world!—are justice and compassion banished from all bosoms ?—seek them, Zoe, in their last shelter, the prison of thy husband! [*exit Zoe*

Must. (aside) Now comes my sentence—I am in a lily dew with apprehension !

Grim. Ho! there—slaves! instantly fetch hither my first cousin the mufti and——

Must. O! that terrible kinsman! thou injured excellence! by all our past tenderness——

Grim. Hold! on second thoughts, prepare my palanquin—I shall go forth myself—[*exeunt slaves*]—*(aside)* Coolness upon this occasion will be more dignified than rage.—Mustapha! go thou strait into the little dark chamber under the moat—seat thyself upon the high three-legged stool in its furthest corner, and there await in thoughtful silence my return!—go!

Must. (sighing dolefully) Oh! [*exit Mustapha*

Grim. Yes; I'll now visit my amiable friend, Grumnildra, and consult with her upon this afflicting subject. As our wrongs are mutual, so may be our vengeance. O! these husbands! these husbands!—ah! the world will never be well managed, till women make the laws and men have only to obey them.

[*exit*

SCENE III—*a room in the prison.*

ALEXIS *discovered.*

Alex. Of all the undone varlets in Bagdat, Alexis the greek, surely thou art the most disconsolate !—in one fatal day I have lost my liberty, my camel, and my wife. Shall I ever recover either of the three ? alas ! no: liberty is like one of my wine flasks, pick but the tiniest crevice through its side and drop by drop all the precious spirit oozes away. The law has lain hold of my camel, and that's a hand never known to relax its grasp while a substance remains to be squeezed ; then for my wife ! not one visit, not one message. Heigho ! all the world seems to have forgotten me, except my gaoler when he unlocks the creaking door of my cell with one hand, and presents with the other, a slice of mouldy bread sopped in a pitcher of brackish water. In a month's time I shall be dieted into the delicate slenderness of an eel, and Zoe will hardly know me for the plump, sleek, well-fed camel driver whom she once regarded. But why do I think of her who has ceased to think of me ? heigho ! ah, the outer grating unlocks——

Zoe. (*without*) Lead me to his cell directly !

Alex. Ha ! Zoe's voice !—she's true, she's true !—Zoe remembers her husband, and Alexis is no longer unhappy !

enter ZOE, *who flies to him.*

Zoe. My husband ! my dearest husband ! I am come to share your dwelling ; have you room for me ?

Alex. In my heart, Zoe ! ever. The pain it has suffered in your absence, teaches it how to value your return.

Zoe. Trust me, mine has not grieved me less bitterly in the interval ; but my delay has not been a neglectful one. I knew, Alexis, that without money in a prison, you must lack many little comforts ; so, I bethought me, to sell the few trinkets my parents left

E

me and supply you from the produce. I had believed the trifles valuable, because they were remembrances from those I loved, but alas ! my hard purchasers rated them by a different estimate, so the sum is very scanty ;—but such as it is, Alexis, despise it not for Zoe's sake.

Alex. (*grasping her hand with emotion*) Zoe, kind, generous Zoe !

Zoe. Nay, now I look about me, I protest a prison seems no such ill dwelling ; only to be sure it bears an ugly name. Courage, dear Alexis ! custom will soon reconcile us to the change. Our acquaintance cannot visit us, but we will make a universe of each other ;—we will talk, sing, and dance together : and trust me, even in bondage, we'll live cheerily.

Alex. (*struggling with his tears*) That will we, girl! live cheerily ? ay ! we'll be happy ; quite happy. Oh ! thumb-screws and bow strings for that damnable cadi ! is there no redress ? can't I petition his superior magistrate, the emir ?

Zoe. Poor fellow ! I dare not tell him all, twould make him desperate. (*aside*) No, no, we have nothing to hope from the *justice* of our oppressors.

Alex. Shall rascality then deride its victims ?—o ! I shall run mad !

Zoe. Alexis ! do I possess your confidence ? I mean your implicit, your unlimited confidence ?

Alex. I were a pagan else !

Zoe. Hear me. I have devised a scheme, but dare not execute it, without your voluntary sanction. Say, will my husband authorise his wife to become an adventuress ?

Alex. If the request had been an impropriety, Zoe could not have preferred it. I place my honor freely in your hands.

Zoe. Thanks, thanks ! the sacred trust shall be returned to its owner unsullied from my use. Your words have inspired me with a new life, and now I fly to my adventure.

Alex. Well—but—hey—how ! am I not to be told.

Zoe. Not one syllable. Without a little mystery, a woman would lack the spur to enterprise. Only remember this ; by to morrow's dawn either Alexis quits this prison to live with Zoe, or Zoe returns to bondage and dies with her Alexis !   [*exit Zoe*

Alex. Farewell ! oh, what a blessing is a good wife, and one that never talks but to the purpose. Ah ! how different is my Zoe to cousin Michael's wife. She deafened the miller, banged the brazier, and buried the undertaker.

SONG.

Bagdat is the place for fun,
    Wo, ho, my camels ;
Four long streets there meet in one,
    Man has his tramels ;
In corner one, poor Hassan fagg'd,
In corner two a miller lagg'd ;
    Whose noisy mill, was never still,
    Its whirling cogs, like barking dogs,
      Went clack, clack, clack ;
Till the poor elf, beside himself,
Cried in a pet, o ! Mahomet,
    Confound all corner houses,
    Confound all corner houses.

At corner three, alas ! alas !
    Wo, ho, my camels,
Dwelt a brazier banging brass,
    Man has his tramels ;
An undertaker at his door,
Thump'd coffin plates at corner four,
Till left and right, from morn till night,
Before, behind, with every wind,
    Clack, clack, bang, bang, rat, tat, tat ;
And the poor elf, beside himself,
Cried in a pet, o ! Mahomet,
    Confound all corner houses,
    Confound all corner houses.

Hassan weary of his life,
 Wo, ho, my camels,
Took unto himself a wife,
 Man has his tramels;
The miller and the brazier stop,
The undertaker shuts up shop,
But when his mate, begins to prate,
She sets the train, to work again,
 With her clack, bang. rat, tat, tat:
Till the poor elf, beside himself,
Cried in a pet, o! Mahomet,
 Confound all talking spouses!
 Confound all talking spouses!

SCENE IV—*a street in Bagdat.*

enter BENMOUSSAFF *and one of his officers.*

Ben. Get you to the prison, and bid the gaoler watch that knave narrowly: keep him on bread and water, that's a very pretty refreshment for a malefactor. And hark'ye! observe particularly that he be kept apart from the other prisoners, for his conversation is dangerous. He might asperse my sacred reputation, and if such rabble once begin with my character——

Officer. Ay, then indeed, your worship, there's no guessing when they would stop. [*exit officer*

Ben. I think I have managed this affair like a refined politician. I have tempted my underling to be dishonest, and pocketed the fruits of his peculation myself; then in due time, the paltry agent is consigned to punishment, while the dignified principal escapes suspicion.

enter ZOE, *behind.*

Zoe. Kind lady fortune! my game is sprung already. Cadi! are you not a barbarous man?

Ben. Oho! my fair mistress disdain, are you with me? you come to importune, but I am marble, perfect adamant. So go thy ways.

126

Zoe. This to Zoe? this to her who but yester-evening you swore was sovereign of your heart.

Ben. Cockatrice! my love is turned to hate.

Zoe. Indeed! well—well! perfidious as thou art; my too easy yielding meets a just rebuke.

Ben. Eh! how? yielding! didst thou say? why, Zoe——

Zoe. No, no, I thank you for this indifference, it restores me to my duty.

Ben. (*aside*) Tis so. I thought my person would secure the day. Ravishing hesitation! does my Zoe then at last relent?

Zoe. Tis of no consequence; your love is turned to hate.

Ben. Adorable creature! my passion is intense as ever. Now I perceive it all;—that cursed blustering husband made you fearful to reveal your sentiments—but, Mahomet be praised! he is kept securely. Say, when may I visit you, shall it be this evening?

Zoe. Saint Athanasius defend me! I admit a male visitor in the evening, alone by myself and unprotected!—this evening, indeed! no, no, not a creature will I suffer to cross my threshold—at least not before midnight.

Ben. The very hour for tenderness! at midnight be it. No impertinent neighbors will then be peeping from their lattices; and old Grumnildra will be snoring. I shall be punctual.

Zoe. No, no, dont come. I have not wherewithal to entertain guests, and my poverty leaves no room for love.

Ben. The Indies are upon your ankles, the Persian Gulf is about your neck, the coast of Barbary, binds your wrists, and the islands of the Archipelago dangle from your ears!—nations shall be ransacked of their treasures to adorn my love. Here's a purse with fifty pieces, to provide some trifling banquet for to-night! say, my mountain snow-flake, dost thou melt at last?

Zoe Ay! even as my countrywoman Danae did to Jupiter of old. (*clinks the purse*) A golden shower is

E 2

the readiest dissolvent in nature !—but soft ! I see my husband's young kinsman, Constantine, at the corner of the street ; dont let him notice us together. Away !

Ben. I fly !—but oh ! the lingering hours ! my love, adieu ! remember twelve, and think of thy Benmous- saff !   [*exit Benmoussaff*

enter CONSTANTINE.

Const. So, cousin ! I perceive you have opened the campaign in earnest.

Zoe. Ay, Constantine ! " and if my young lieutenant has but prospered equally with his general in the onset, the foe shall be routed horse and foot." Say, dear coz, hast entangled Mustapha ?

Const. Nay, trust me, I am not so young but I can execute a lady's commands with adroitness ;—though, faith, I had a plaguy trouble to manage the affair. Old Grimnigra had but just forgiven her caitiff, and they were cooing together like a brace of turtles after a thunder storm ; so I was forced to feign business of state, before I could speak to him in private.

Zoe. Well, coz, what said he to my message ?

Const. Oh! I can't remember half ;—but here—you may read what he has written. (*gives a billet*)

Zoe. (*reads*) " Composed of spices, and distillation of all fragrant gums ! thy obsequious vassal sendeth greeting ! thy kinsman's words have dispersed all doubt ; thou didst suspect my termagant wife in her hiding-place, and therefore in prudence didst affect aversion from my suit. I will visit thee after midnight— even as thou hast appointed—till when, forget not thy adoring Mustapha." Excellent !

Const. So say I, for this purse accompanies the note, that a proper feast may be prepared for his reception.

Zoe. Oh, the munificence of these withered gallants ! but I am already supplied for the night's entertainment —so carry Mustapha's present to my husband's gaoler, discharge the penalty for which he is confined, and leave directions that he be liberated by to-morrow's dawn ;·but remember, he must not know of his release *before* to-morrow.

Const. Ah! now you task me with a gladsome service.

Zoe. I shall find you more errands anon—therefore I charge you despatch this commission quickly.

Const. Think you I could loiter upon such an embassy ; the herald of liberty, like the courier of love, should post it upon wings as light and frolic as the news he bears ! [*exit Zoe*] ah, me !´dark-eyed Oneiza expects me this evening. Well, twill be my first trespass, and when I name its cause, the generous girl will absolve her rover.

AIR—CONSTANTINE.

My dark-eyed maid ! by moonlight hour
Thou'lt seek alone our wonted bower ;
Thy hand of snow will strew the ground
With balmy leaves and blossoms round,
And oft two lips of flame will sigh,
" Forgetful lover ! art thou nigh ?"
Then, as the night-breeze stirs a bough—
" I hear his step—he hastens now !"
  Alas ! for hopes by fate betrayed,
  No lover seeks his dark eyed maid !

My dark-eyed maid ! then wilt thou weep,
And sigh and sob thy heart to sleep—
Should fancy tempt thee with a dream,
She but renews thy waking theme ;
And thou wilt murmur words of bliss,
And pout thy lips to print a kiss—
And stretch thy circling arms in air,
And seem to clasp thy lover there !
  Alas ! for dreams by fate betrayed,
  No lover clasps his dark-eyed maid !   [*exit*

SCENE v—*the gardens of the seraglio.*

the ÆTHIOP *enters, waving his ebony wand, followed by* ALMANZOR *and* ORASMYN.

Alm. Wondrous man ! with fresh amaze at each´

new pace I follow thee, through close-drawn barriers and the watch of guards, that wand, unchallenged still directs a way.   Where stand we now?

Æth. Even in the gardens of Alraschid's palace ;—here, at the sultry hour, it ever is Cephania's custom, 'midst these spicy shades, where palms and cedars half exclude the day, and fountains bubble in sequestered freshness, to muse alone and commune with her god. -

Oras. Ah! may I then behold my sister?

Æth. Hither have I led thee to that special joy ;—days, months, nay, years, still shrouded by my spells, here have I paced, and gazed, and wished ; ne'er daring by a sigh to hint my presence.   *Thou,* unreproved, shall clasp her angel form, twine 'midst her arms and grow into her heart !—happy Orasmyn ! ha ! my love appears !—lo ! ye—glorious as fresh day through severing shades, she breaks from yon close cypress walk.

Alm. By allah !— her royal father's port—o ! memory!——

CEPHANIA *is seen traversing the distance of the scene.*

Æth. Soft ye awhile ; Orasmyn first, *alone,* addresses her : the brother's and the sister's earliest words should meet no witness, save great nature's ear.—Young prince ! this bower will veil thee till a fitting moment. (*places him in one of the forward scenes*) She comes—this way a while.

(*he withdraws Almanzor down an opposite walk—at the same moment Cephania appears upon a bridge over a piece of artificial water which divides the garden*)

Ceph. (*from the bridge*) Immyne, command my train they wait at distance. (*plaintive music till she reaches the front*) At length I am alone—a moment now is mine for thought, for meditation, for despair ! yes, yes, *despair!* no single ray of hope is left to cheer my destiny ! o, ye dear combatants ! whichever of you lives the victor, Cephania's eyes must weep against some grave she rather would have made her own — Come, inexorable doom of all my joys ! dear, yet detested cypher ! come, and once more teach me all my wretchedness ! (*she reads the paper given to her by the arab*) " beloved niece, the bonds of thy captivity shall soon be broken. That brother, whom in infancy report had slain, yet truly lives to claim his birthright and avenge his race ; this night Orasmyn enters Bagdat : the slave who tenders this can fully name our plans and teach thee how to aid their arm. Learn this in brief ! the tyrant husband who hath forced thy vows is doomed a certain victim of thy kinsmen's swords.— Thine, most tenderly, Almanzor." O what a wayward spite is here ! mad contradiction of our stars ! at once my boon and bane are prophecied. Thou dear brother ! for thee an ancient throne is reared ;—thou dearer husband ! an untimely grave is dug for thee !— my poor distracted heart is torn between you !—perchance, while yet I ponder, some dreadful act is shaping ; nay, fix thee, my wavering spirit ! make thy decision quickly ; which shall I save, which sacrifice ?— how, if I betray the plot and so preserve Alraschid ?— ah ! what fiend so damned shall lend me eyes to watch a brother's and an uncle's agony, broken and quivering upon fiery wheels and howling curses with their dying breath ?—the thought is horror ! nay, then, to join their cause and so—allah ! live I to dream it ?— murder my husband ? no, no—that way madness lies ! (*she suddenly kneels with fervor*) o thou, who art in paradise ! my father once, my guardian spirit still— thee I adjure ! (*takes a miniature from her bosom*) behold thy wretched daughter, now gazing on the treasured copy of thy living looks. Father, father ! endow this senseless ivory with some quick charm ;— bid these fixed eyes express my duty, breathe through these silent lips thine awful will. Father ! save thy child ! (*Orasmyn, with a stealing step, advances from the bower, and tremulously kneels at Cephania's side —her eye suddenly perceives his figure, and she gazes fearfully*) guard me, allah ! what lovely apparition's this ?—eyes, see you truly ? or is't illusion all ? (*Orasmyn silently raises her hand to his lips, and bursts*

131

into tears upon it) nay, the touch is warm and human —and now, quick natural tears are gushing on my hand. Speak, gentle youth, who art thou ? (*the boy, unable to articulate, points to the miniature in her hand*) ha ! (*she looks alternately from the picture to the boy*) dear sacred eyes !—nay, ye beam reflected *here* !—my father's sweet yet serious smile !—tis truly copied by a living lip. Can it be ?—no, no—and yet —*Orasmyn ?*

Oras. Sister ! sister ! (*the boy extends his arms— Cephania shrieks and drops into his embrace*)

Ceph. Ha ! I have thee at my heart, thou last dear relic of my royal house ! nay, let me gaze for ever on those looks ; trace the dead father in the living son —call round me phantoms of departed years, and lose my miseries in a golden dream !

Oras. And has my sister thought of her Orasmyn ? have those sweet eyes bewept my fancied loss ?—and do they glitter now to view me safe ?

Ceph. (*starting*) Safe ! safe !—nay, *art* thou safe ? doth Ali's son seek safety here ? o my gay trance dis- solves ;—thou dearest, richest treasure of my soul ! what fatal planet hath betrayed thy steps, and lured thee here to bondage or to death ?

Oras. Believe me, I am safe ; in truth I am ;—a power beyond my rival's guards my way   I view thee pale and trembling for my fate, if captured by Alras- chid ; now I guess a sister's sufferings ;—dry those streaming eyes. Orasmyn's sword shall pay their tears with blood ! this arm is destined to avenge our race.

Ceph. Ha ! talk'st thou of revenge and death ?—ye gods ! can hellish thoughts lurk in so fair an ambush ? kind, lovely boy, say I mistook thy speech. Can lips so smiling thirst for blood ? ah ! whose ?

Oras. Alraschid's ; false, usurping, cruel tyrant ! that smothering torch, which all my kinsman's fury had not breath to rouse, those piteous sighs have light- ed into flame ; have I a heart, and lacks it warmth to kindle at a sister's wrongs ? beloved Cephania ! no, by earth and heaven I swear! Alraschid falls by thine Orasmyn's arm!

Ceph. Inhuman boy! first plant thy poniard here.

Oras. How says my sister?

Ceph. Oh! I abjure that name; are wo and widowhood a brother's gift? thou rash, deceived distracting youth! learn that I love the man thou think'st I hate; by holiest passion, not a tyrant's power, the glorious, generous Alraschid reigns, throned in my heart, and lord of all its fires!

Oras. Amazing words!

Ceph. Hear me; when first I wore his conquering father's chain, the gallant prince in secret soothed a little orphan's wo; and even while I strove to hate him, stole my love. Scarce had the sceptre to his hand devolved, ere knelt the monarch at his bondsmaid's feet, " daughter of Ali!" cried he, " our sires in life were foes; o! be their hatred buried with their dust, and let the diadem they crossly claimed be shared in friendship by their gentler heirs!"

Oras. Could such pure justice be a tyrant's act?

Ceph. Brand not my hero with a term so foul: all Bagdat blesses his paternal care, and *father of his people* is the glorious boast, that crowns his name beyond a Cæsar's empty vaunt! to reign, is nothing: but to reign *beloved*, is god's true copy and the type of heaven!

Oras. Your words amaze! confound, distract me; ah! wherefore have I sworn to slay this man?

Ceph. Sworn! just gods! what fatal oath——

Oras. Ay! tis rightly termed—a *fatal* oath indeed! but earth heard and heaven hath recorded it; our father's awful ghost is witness to my pledge!

Ceph. Distraction! misery! what dæmon tempted thee to sin so deep?

Oras. Oh! twas a dark, dreadful being; but one so powerful, so *very* powerful, I dare not thwart his will——

Ceph. Disclose the wretch, that with some sudden curse——

Oras. (*grasps her hand tremulously*) Hush ! hush! perchance he hears us now——

Ceph. Ha ! where is the slave concealed ?

Oras. Nay, hush ! (*he looks fearfully around—at that instant the* ÆTHIOP *emerges from concealing trees and stands before him*) ah ! behold him ; there ! there !

Ceph. (*gazing indignantly*) Fiend abhorred ! thou subtle tempter of ingenuous youth ! now let my nimble curses strike and——

ALMANZOR *steps forward to the Æthiop's side, and takes his hand.*

Ah ! what silver-headed seer is he, who knits his ancient palm to hellish hands, and lends a reverend sanction to the damned ? say it is not—in mercy ! *not* Almanzor——

Alm. (*advancing*) Beloved niece !

Ceph. Avaunt ! for now I curse my birth, my being ; and all kindred blood ! fell murderer ! wouldst thou ? no, no, that heart was once so kind. (*she suddenly casts herself at his feet*) Behold ! I clasp thy knees and bathe them with my tears ! dear venerable man ! prove thou art still my uncle, and say thou hast not leagued against my husband's life !

Alm. Is this my welcome ? dost thou plead for him and by a husband's name ? my age is choleric—be wary how its fires are stirred ! husband ! husband ! (*grasps Cephania's hand, and drags her towards the Æthiop*) forget that name for ever, or address it—here !

Ceph. (*recoiling wildly*) To plague and to contagion rather ! gods ! do I dream ! brain ! brain ! start not quite—(*she presses her forehead between her hands for an instant, and then addresses rapidly with a desperate look and accent*) men ! men ! one brief word decides the fate of all ; speak ! is murder your resolve ?

Alm. By allah ! yea ! this night Alraschid dies !

Ceph. Nay, then I know my course ! (*calling aloud*) my guards !

Oras. (*rushing to her*) Sister ! would'st thou betray——

Ceph. Hence ! hence ! let slaughter revel in my house's blood ! I doom ye all to save a husband : guards ! guards !

Alm. (*drawing a dagger*) Unnatural traitress !

Æth. (*catching his arm*) Forbear ! although countless thousands wait her call, no eye, save singly hers, may find our forms. (*snatches Cephania s hand, and kisses it fervently*) Glorious fair ! thus in her rage and fury do I woo my love !

Ceph. Ruffian ! avaunt—help ! help !

Æth. Yet once again ! now hail, Cephania ! hail, the Æthiop's bride !

Ceph (*tearing herself from his embrace*) Guards ! help ! help ! (*the Æthiop waving his wand triumphantly withdraws his companions into the bower—at the same moment, the women and slaves of the sultana rush in all directions forward, and surround their mistress*)

Im Gracious lady ! whence these cries ?

Ceph. Advance ! enter yon bower and quickly seize: yet hold ! (*she hesitates*) gods ! what would I do ? destroy a brother's life ? horror ! horror !

Im. Merciful allah ! convulsive terrors shake you.

Ceph. (*attempting to collect herself*) As I reposed within yon bower, a serpent crawled upon my seat, unawares ; the reptile startled me, but I escaped its bite.

Im. Swift let your slaves explore the bower, and—

Ceph. (*flings herself between them*) Hold ! I charge you on your lives forbear ! perchance its sting were mortal ; no, let the monster peacefully depart : this quarter of the gardens shall awhile be quitted. Immyne ! lend thine arm and lead me hence—let all retire with me. (*Cephania leads the way, when the Æthiop leading forth his companions appears at the entrance of the bower*)

Ceph. (*starting*) Madness and ruin ! why are ye seen ? hence ! hence ! begone !

F

Im. Lady !

Ceph. (*turning to her train half-frenzied*) Betray them not ! whate'er their crime, forbear ! nay, I command you let them freely pass.

Im. Whom ? gracious queen !

Ceph. These three imprudent strangers. (*slaves all look around them rapidly, and in apparent consternation*)

Im. Where, lady may we seek them ?

Ceph. Gods ! they approach—there ! there !

Im. (*looking as Cephania's finger points*) I only can perceive the citron tree, scattering its blossoms as the zephyr stirs it. (*the Æthiop leading his companions, passes slowly out of sight, while Cephania, gasping and wonder struck, sustains herself by Immyne's arm*)

Ceph. (*after a pause*) Infernal powers ! can ye work so cunningly. Immyne ! thou art right ; now my eyes are clear again ; twas but the quaint illusion of a feverish brain !

Im. Beloved mistress ! you are faint and pale ; the recent terror has disturbed your mind.

Ceph. It hath in truth Immyne ! give me a moment's pause to collect my spirits. (*aside*) This night the blow is threatened. What if I seek Alraschid instantly, win by tears and prayers a solemn promise of his mercy ere I breathe the tale, and then——

GIAFAR *is seen traversing the garden.*

Im. Lady ! the vizier hastens to your presence.

Giaf. Sultana ! the great Alraschid sends me to your feet. Our royal master, not less renowned for piety than valor, laboring to avert the prophet's wrath from this offending land, hath imposed upon himself a solemn penance ; and now within his chamber is locked in solitary prayer : it is enjoined that till to-morrow's dawn, no earthly form or voice obtrude between his lifted soul and heaven !

Ceph. (*aside*) Disastrous chance ! not till to-morrow, said you ?

Giaf. Even so, lady ! hath the caliph sworn:

Ceph. (*aside*) To morrow !—ah, Alraschid ! never may that morrow dawn for *thee !* might I confide in Giafar ? no, no, the viziers all are hostile to my race ; only with Alraschid lies my hope.   Giafar ! I grieve that I must break the caliph's law, but an affair of moment leads me to his presence.

Giaf. Lady ! forgive the lowliest of your servants if he bars your way ; you are my revered mistress ever ; but I am sworn upon this duty, and dare not quit my oaths.

Ceph. (*proudly*) This to Cephania ! I am forgotten sure !—but mark me, lord ! behold this ring ! all may remember on my bridal day, Alraschid drew the sparkling circlet on my finger and by a lover's strongest vow engaged his faith, whenever I gave or sent it back, to yield whatever suit of mine accompanied the pledge. Now, officious lord ! stand I still forbidden ?—ha !

Giaf. (*bowing respectfully*) I recognise my sovereign's pledge, and may not interdict the claim it vouches.

Ceph. Immyne ! bear with thy utmost speed this jewel to the caliph, none dare question such a passport, and in Cephania's name demand an instant interview.

[*exit Immyne*

Giaf. Forgive my honest zeal ; but lady, sure some strange disorder shakes your frame. Alas ! what secret grief ; might Giafar presume——

Ceph. (*aside*) His keen suspicious eyes look through me ; nay, I must counterfeit. You are mistaken ; my spirits hold their tenor evenly ; nay, I could be joyous ! come ! let sports and pleasures crown the hour—here will I rest awhile. (*slaves advance, and place cushions in the form of a throne, on which Cephania reclines— Giafar follows the direction of her hand, and stands by her side*) Now let my slaves exert their skill. (*a ballet is commenced by the female slaves of the sultana—suddenly, distant cries of* pursue ! pursue ! *interrupt the festivity—the* ARAB, *who appeared in the first scene, is perceived flying across the extremity of the garden followed by guards—he bursts through the dancers, who shriek and disperse—a massive chain fastened to his left wrist drags after him—panting and breathless he gains the front)*

Arab. Save me ' *(sees Cephania)* ha ! you will— yes, yes, you will save me ! *(flings himself before her)*

Ceph. (rising) Great allah ! tis the very arab : yea, he who but yester morning——

Giaf. (aside) Confusion ! escaped ! and with Cephania !—sultana ! hear him not ;—guards ! drag him hence !

Arab. No, no ; daughter of Ali ! guard thy kinsman's slave :—I have burst my cell, outflown my guards, and fate itself directs me to thy feet.

Giaf. (to guards) Advance !

Ceph Nay, hold ! it is your queen's command !— arab ! thou art safe—declare thy grievance.

Arab. Angel ! racks have extorted from my quivering lips words dearer than my life ; but hear me yet, and all may be repaired——

Ceph Speak !

IMMYNE, *who has been seen returning during the latter speeches. now gains the front, and instantly casts herself between the arab and Cephania.*

Im. Sultana ! with mercy view your trembling slave !

Ceph. Immyne !

Im. The ring ! the *ring !* just as I reached the royal chamber to present the pledge. a hand unknown grasped mine, and suddenly the jewel vanished !

Ceph. Where is the traitor who has dared——

the ÆTHIOP *rushes to the bridge in the centre of the stage, and exultingly displays the ring.*

Ah ! tis he, tis *he !*—the dreadful one ! *(the Æthiop scornfully smiles and fixes it on his finger)* despair ! despair ! *(she sinks back insensible upon the cushions)*

Giaf Ha ! she faints !—triumphant chance ! *(to guards)* swift seize your prisoner—NOW !

Arab. (struggling) Forbear !—sultana ! mistress !

Giaf. She hears not, helps not, away ! (*the guards drag the arab backward, while the women cluster about the throne, where their mistress lies insensible—the Æthiop remains in the posture of exultation, and the curtain falls upon the scene*)

END OF THE SECOND ACT.

ACT III.

SCENE I—*an inner cell of the catacombs.*

enter ORASMYN, *as from the principal vault, followed by the* ÆTHIOP, *who bears the poniard from the altar.*

Oras. Away, away! remorseless being ! pursue me not to damn me.

Æth. Infatuated boy ! I follow to preserve thee !— whither would'st thou fly ?

Oras. To my native desert. The tenants of the wilderness are savage, but man, social man is more inexorable far !—oh ! if pity ever dawned upon that dark bosom, permit my flight, while yet these hands are undefiled with blood !

Æth. Fantastic scruples !—shrinks thy nice conscience at a just revenge, and dreads it not some direr penalty for broken sacraments and deities adjured in vain ?—thine oath ! prince ! think upon thine oath !

Oras. I do, with horror, with despair !

enter ALMANZOR, *from behind.*

Alm. How, now ! wherefore have you thus withdrawn from our assembled friends ; they call upon their prince ;—haste, Orasmyn, and rejoin them ere they quit the altar. (*some few notes of a religious chant strike on the ear*) Hark ! the last dread covenant now murmurs on their lips.

F 2

Oras. Would I were in my grave!

Æth. Beware the doom entailed on perjured heads! (*he passes the boy's hands to Almanzor*) Our conference concludes. My friends! complete your vows, then pass undaunted to the glorious act that crowns this scheme of wonders; the fatal minutes speed: one little hour yet scarce remains to shade and silence, ere flames and groans demand the rest of night. Is our muster perfect? hath each leader conned his separate charge?

Alm. By thy strict counsels all our plan is framed. Hassan fires the bezestein. Abudah storms the tower beyond. Orasmyn, by myself accompanied, assails Alraschid.

Æth. Ay! *thou* art his comrade, only *thou*: my cha s would else prove vain.

Alm. Enough! I pant for vengeance—come!

Æth Soft ye! one moment yet; here, dear confederates we part.

Alm. How say you! part?

Æth We sunder here, to meet in triumph, or to meet no more. A living Ali only may revenge the Ali lost; so destiny decrees! lo! ye, the farewell gifts my friendship hath prepared—this poniard and this wand! (*gives the poniard to Orasmyn, and the wand to Almanzor*) employ them rightly, and success is yours.

Alm. Hold! while linked with thee each daring wonder seems an easy task, whose power is stronger than the kings of earth; but thy mysterious aid withdrawn—

Æth. Doubt not, unseen, unheard, my watchful spirit still shall guard your course; my spells already bind Alraschid's guards in an unstirring sleep: the wand securely leads you to the tyrant's couch. My second gift, Orasmyn guesses how to use.

Alm. Our spirits stand confirmed! away to vengeance!

Æth. To fame, to glory, and a hero's joys! farewell! the watchful Æthiop still protects your way.

[*exeunt separately*

SCENE II—*inside of Alexis's cabin—a banquet set out with lights.*

enter ZOE, *brilliantly habited, and* CONSTANTINE.

Zoe. Speed! speed! good cousin; make all in readiness for my illustrious guests : do not my fine robes become me?

Const. Oh! you look and move to a miracle.   Mercy on the hearts of all emirs and cadies.   I vow I tremble for myself: nay, I dare gaze no longer!

Zoe. Away, you flatterer, hie to your post; and have a care my visitors are introduced with due ceremony. Away! [*exit Constantine*] methinks I tread on air, and all my nimble spirits spring to the adventure! (*knocking without*) punctual to the moment! oh! were our magistrate but as brisk in his duties as his amours, who would complain of the law's delay?

Constantine ushers in BENMOUSSAFF.

Ben. Constellation! human wonder! is it mere earthly woman I behold, or some unsteady star just fallen from the sphere?

Zoe. Pure flesh and blood, I assure your worship; but had I been one of the heavenly bodies you talk of, I might indeed have fallen if such a seducer had attracted me to earth.

Ben. Extatic moment! oh! I can't sustain it; I'm all in a soft delirium lost——

Zoe. I have provided a poor banquet for your entertainment: come, let me invite your worship to partake! (*they sit with great ceremony*) nay, each shall carve for the other; the viands will be doubly relished when mutually presented by the hand we love!

Ben. Was there ever such an engaging creature! (*aside*) she is distractedly fond; I can read in her eyes the vehemence of her passion.

Zoe. (*filling a goblet with wine, touches it with her lip, and then passes it to Benmoussaff*) I drink to the health of him whom I adore! will your worship pledge me?

Ben. Wine! Mahomet forbids it.

Zoe. Zoe recommends it!

Ben. Enough! thou art my new faith, and thus I wash down the scruples of my old. *(drinks)* I protest it tickles and tingles marvellously. Nay, tis a very innocent cordial. *(drinks)* It cheereth the heart of man and; nay, tis your only drink for elegant gallantry. *(drinks again)* Fair Zoe! I entreat one boon, a chaste salute!

Zoe. Fy! fy! so early, your worship.

Ben. Nay, prithee! aha! I must, I will—*(a second knocking)*

Zoe. Hold! somebody knocks.

Ben. Some idle boys, I'll have them ducked in the Tygris.

enter CONSTANTINE.

Const. Oh! cousin, cousin! I vow here's the emir, Mustapha, at the gate—seeing lights and hearing voices at this unusual hour, he insists upon entering and searching the house for suspicious characters.

Ben. Search the house! I would not be found by him in it for a kiss round the caliph's haram. He's my sworn enemy, and out of very malice would report our intrigue to my wife, and then——*(knocks again)*

Const. There, hear how impatient! what's to be done?

Zoe. I have it: your worship can lay concealed for a minute in one of these chests that have brought home my fine new clothes. The emir finding the apartment vacant will depart satisfied directly.

Ben. A magistrate squeezed into a chest! what will become of my dignity?

Zoe. You shall take it along with you; twill lie in a narrow compass. *(he gets into the chest)*

Ben. But Zoe, should he look into the chest.

Zoe. *(squeezing him down)* To prevent that, I'll fasten the lid. *(turns the key and takes it out)* Ha! ha!

oh! cupid! what a triumph. Myrtle-chains may en-
tangle some lovers, but for mine, I prefer the security
of a lock and key.

Constantine introduces MUSTAPHA.

Must. My fair mistress Zoe. Thus doth the lofty-
one prostrate himself. (*kneels*) Here let me plead my
passion in accents tuneful as the turtle's wail. Ugh!
ugh! by the way waiting so long at your door in the
night-air, has brought on my winter cough.

Zoe. I protest, my lord, I am very sorry; but my
neighbors are so watchful I was fearful of admitting
you, till I had ascertained no spy was lurking under
the wall.

Must. I applaud your precaution, it behoves us to be
circumspect in the management of our amour; that
wife of mine, but in sight of heaven I'll not mention
the devil. So that despicable old mummy Benmoussaff affected to address you, eh? the ridiculous vanity of some men! but you treated him as he deserved.

Zoe. I hope so, my lord.

Must. The wretch is my antipathy; he is positively
a walking horror, and ought to be shut up for life;
dont you agree with me?

Zoe. Perfectly, my lord, " *shut up for life,*" is my
very sentence!

Ben. (*from the chest*) Oh!

Must. What's that?

Zoe. Only an echo: the very walls and furniture
agree with our opinion. (*knocking without*)

Must. That's another echo! what's that?

Zoe. I am as ignorant as yourself. (*aside*) Sure they
have not arrived so early.

enter CONSTANTINE *frightened.*

Const. (*aside to Zoe*) Oh! dear cousin, dont be an-
gry with me, but such an accident——

Zoe. What? what?

Const. When I took the money for Alexis's release,

I forgot to tell the gaoler to detain him till next morning ; and he is now at the gate.

Zoe. Undone ! undone ! you have ruined me ! his impetuous temper will mar every thing.

Must. Eh ! how ! what's the affair ? you seem terrified

Zoe. Truly I have cause : my husband is now without the gate.

Must. Would I were in the same situation. Cockatrice ! you have plotted this to abuse me.

Zoe. No ! by every sacred name I swear I was ignorant till this very moment of his release from prison. (*knocking repeated*)

Alex. (*without*) Why, Zoe, wife, house !

Must. What's to be done: if he enters I'm ruined !

Zoe. Speak to him through the casement, Constantine, and make some excuse to send him away.

Const. What shall I say ?

Zoe Say I am ill, very ill.

Must. (*in his fright*) Yes, I am very ill.

Const. (*through casement at side scene*) Dear cousin, pray go away for a while. Zoe is very ill.

Alex. (*without*) Ill ! and I not with her ! open instantly.

Zoe. No, no, tell him I am at my prayers.

Must. I'll begin mine this moment.

Const. No, she's not ill ; but she's at her prayers.

Zoe. (*prompting him*) And must not be disturbed.

Const. And must not be disturbed.

Alex. Young traitor, this is false.

Zoe. (*forgetting herself puts her head out*) I tell you it's true: I'm at my prayers, and must not be disturbed.

Alex. The devil you are ! now then, if my foot can split a door——

Zoe. Hold ! hold ! it shall be opened to you. Oh, my lord ! you must conceal yourself.

Must. (*in violent alarm*) Where ? where ?

Zoe. Here luckily is an empty chest ; in, in.

Must. But when shall I get out ?

Zoe. No words ; I'll provide for your release. (*she fastens him in*) Oh ! this unlucky return ! if Alexis had been confined but one hour longer, all my projects would have stood secure, but his temper is so violent——

enter ALEXIS.

Alex. So. I am admitted to my own house at last ; I hope I dont interrupt my wife's devotions too early. (*he sees the banquet and lights, then Zoe in her splendid dress, as she advances with a smile to receive him*) Am I awake ? no, no, I dream ; at least I hope so. Is this a camel-driver's cabin, this the wife of his poverty ?

Zoe. Now spirit of my sex, befriend me ! welcome, Alexis ! welcome ! how ! you reject my hand ? are you not glad to see me ?

Alex. I cannot speak to her. Zoe ! ought I to receive your hand ? is it the same pure hand I pressed at parting ? go ! go ! I know it not ; tis disguised in jewels.

Zoe. The ring you gave me at the altar is among them.

Alex. Oh, Zoe! Zoe ! do not distract me. Have you, I cannot bear the thought ; explain these riddles or you break my heart. (*he flings himself into a chair*)

Zoe. Poor fellow ! but I must still dissemble. What is it you would inquire ?

Alex. Your dress, these lights, this banquet : what does it mean ?

Zoe. I expect company.

Alex. Fiends and fury ! do you own it to my face ? appoint gallants, and bid your husband witness their reception !

Zoe. I did not impose any such trial of your politeness: you need not stay till my visitors arrive.

Alex. I shall run mad ; nay, sure I am so now. What ! turn the tame cuckold, and draw the curtains on my own dishonor ! no, no ; if my brows must be goaded, let the artificers of horns beware of their point.

(a knocking) Ha! the signal is given; now then for discovery of all.

enter CONSTANTINE.

Alex. (*catching him by the collar*) Ha! thou little infamy! thou egg of baseness cracking in the shell! confess thy treacheries, or look for doomsday suddenly.

Const. Prithee, good cousin, what must I confess?

Alex. Dissimulating imp! these visitors: who are they?

Const. Oh! my cousin Zoe's invited guests.

Alex. Tartarus and the furies! they own it; own it to my face!

Const. Why not? such company bring credit to your door: two of the noblest dames in Bagdat.

Alex. Dames! said you?—dames!

Const. Ay, and stately ones:—the ladies Grimnigra and Grumnildra: the wives of the emir Mustapha and the cadi Benmoussaff, are now in their palanquins at the door.

Alex. Miracles! why Zoe, can this be?

Zoe. I disdain to answer. (*to Constantine*) Usher these illustrious ladies into my presence.

Alex. Women of quality visit a camel driver's wife! where shall I run to 'scape them? how shall I hide me?

Zoe. No, I insist that you remain upon the spot.

enter GRIMNIGRA *and* GRUMNILDRA.

Grim. Well, Zoe, we attend your summons:—my estimable Grumnildra is as impatient as myself to learn the drift of your request.

Grum. Ay, child!—you mention treasures of ours having accidentally fallen into your possession—is't not so?

Zoe. Precisely the case, my ladies.

Alex (*shuffling behind the table*) Oho! a discovered treasure: this explains madam's finery.

Grim. Prithee, Zoe, what uneasy looking man is

that? he, who fidgets about in the corner of the room.

Zoe. Only a person I call husband, my lady : a little awe-struck at your presence.   You perceive he knows his distance.

Grim. I do ; the order you preserve in your household is creditable to your judgment : poor man, let him remain.   Now, to the business : these treasures, Zoe?

Zoe. Are such as your ladyships, doubtless, will deem inestimable ; I hold them at this moment securely under my own lock and key ; and might so detain them unsuspected by any here, but my heart is an honest one and longs for nothing more sincerely than to restore stray chattels into the hands of their real owners.

Grum. Honorable creature !

Grim. A pattern of morals ! I am all curiosity to behold these treasures.

Zoe. Yonder chests contain them.   You will permit my husband to be present while you examine the contents of each, and the keys are at your service.

AIR—ZOE.

These keys can a treasure unfold,
More precious than jewels or gold—
To judge by myself for each wife,
'Tis treasure more worth than her life !
   Then, ladies, advance, yet, soft, prithee stay,
   One word to my husband I first fain would say ;
               Fal lal de ral de ra.

(to Alexis)

These keys can dispense sovereign cure
For torments the jealous endure,
One peep in yon mystical chest
Turns your heart-ache at once to a jest.
   Now, ladies, advance, I present you these keys,
   Dispose of the treasures within as you please ;
               Fal lal de ral de ra.

G

(each wife opens a chest to the last notes of the song—Mustapha and Benmoussuff put up their heads)

Grim. I'm petrified!

Ben. I'm suffocated!

Alex I'm transported!—oh, Zoe, Zoe! *(runs and embraces her)*

Grum. Come forth, thou sensual caitiff!

Grim. Libertine, dislodge! *(they drag their husbands forward)*

Alex. Ha, ha, ha!—all hail, ye venerable Tarquins. Hold, sides, or I shall die. Ha, ha, ha!

Grim. Dost thou expect to survive this mortal affront to my honor?

Must. No; I'm doomed and dead already.

Grum. And thou! by all my injuries I swear——

Ben. Not yet. I'm taken of the sudden strangely. Nay, let me go home; I'm very ill.

Must. I think I feel an odd twinge too.

Grim. Five hundred strokes of the bastinado, administered in the presence of my cousin the mufti, I prescribe for *thee*; my black slaves shall apply the cure.

Grum. Thank heaven, I have an arm that can avenge itself.

Ben. I know it, and I venerate its wondrous mightiness.

Zoe. Ladies, I commend my reverend gallants to your indulgence. Ridicule is the best corrective of the vicious, and perhaps I have drenched my patients with a sufficient dose. Alexis! forgive the momentary trial I made of your temper. Believe me, I probed the wound, only that I might close it with security for ever. Mine is the general cause of wives: if a victory attained by stratagem be honorable among mighty warriors, it cannot be reproachful to a weak unaided woman; and while offended morals are revenged with playfulness, I trust even prudery itself will scarce arraign the justice or the delicacy of Zoe the grecian wife.

SEPTETTO.

Zoe.　　　La lira! la lira!
　　　　　　The battle is done,
　　　　　　A victory won,
　　　And Zoe reigns queen of the field.
Alex.　　　La lira! la lira!
　　　　　　My jealousy flies,
　　　　　　Subdued by those eyes,
　　　Where the banner of faith is reveal'd.
Grim.　　　La lira! la lira!
　　　　　　My wandering love,
　　　　　　Restored to his dove—
Must. From her bosom swears never to roam.
Grum.　　　La lira! la lira!
　　　　　　Men knowing their duty,
　　　　　　Who seek for true beauty—
Ben. Will find the dear angel at home.
Const.　　　La lira! la lira!
　　　　　　Thrice happy the lives
　　　　　　Of husbands and wives,
　　　With such virtues and graces possest.
All.　　　La lira! la lira!
　　　　　　We'll rival the loves
　　　　　　Of the murmuring doves,
　　　And exist but each other to bless.　　[*exeunt*

SCENE III—*a gallery lighted feebly by a lamp, leading to the caliph's apartments.*

enter CEPHANIA *and* IMMYNE.

Ceph. Begone, Immyne! leave me to my fate!

Im My royal mistress! in this distraction? nay, I
dare not quit you thus; tis midnight: wherefore forsake
your couch, to traverse these solitary galleries and
pause at last upon this silent spot?

Ceph. Here, have I reached the goal I sought; this
door conducts by a private passage. to the caliph's
chamber. Giafar's stern command hath barred all other access. Nay, get thee hence; my direful enterprize
admits no aid of thine?

Im. Lady!

Ceph. Now, I command thee—hence! (*Immyne bows and retires*) Yes, my Alraschid! our mutual hour of destiny is come ; we are one, indissolubly *one*. By love and by religion joined, whose arms shall sunder us? not the murderer's ; no, no ; if the fatal blow must fall, through the wife's bosom it assails the husband : one death, one grave, one spirit married to eternity! (*she approaches the door and strikes against it*) ho! who waits within? (*a pause*) ha! no reply! two pages are ever stationed next this door—tis firmly barred within. (*she strikes again more eagerly*) Allah! still this distracting silence. Hath the destroying dagger then already pierced—horror! horror! hear me, Alraschid! (*the closing of a heavy portal sounds from the side of the gallery by which she has advanced*) ah! some closing portal echoes through the gallery, footsteps advance ; yon quivering lamp now gleams upon a figure. Ha! it is, it *is* the murderer's step! sustain me, heaven! father of mercies guard Alraschid! (*she faintly totters to some pillars in the side scene, and conceals herself between them*)

   enter ALMANZOR, *hurrying forward* ORASMYN.

Alm. Swifter, nay, swifter! weak, timid boy! you tremble!

Oras. Well I may! methinks at every step, I wade through streams of blood, and hear some dying groan beneath me!

Alm. Silence, and proceed! (*regarding the door attentively*) yea! tis here we enter, so the Æthiop counselled ; the phœnix dying to revive by fire denotes the portal. Hail! glorious symbol of an empire's fate. So Bagdat's throne by midnight sinks to rise thrice glorious with succeeding morn! come, faithful talisman, complete thy task! (*he strikes against the door with the wand, instantly it springs open and displays upon its inner side, in glaring characters,* " ADVANCE !") the last obedience to our charm is yielded, and lo! a word of inspiration cheers our cause! advance! tis fate's own mighty sign ! haste ! favorite of the stars ! obey the call ! (*he turns to the front where Orasmyn stands gazing upon the sign, as Almanzor approaches him he turns away, and with frenzied earnestness kneels—Almanzor struck with his action, pauses in silence by his side—Cephania at the same time steals forward from her concealment and glides through the door*)

Ceph. Allah ! be my guide !

Oras. Oh ! thou, that in this dark and silent hour, viewest and hearest all things ; nay, readest in the heart that secret thought, lips never yet have matched with sound, be witness that thy kneeling creature. in this tremendous act obeys, but thy command, through seeming oracles declared ! perplexed ! confounded, half distracted ; if through his human ignorance he errs, vouchsafe forgiveness to the witless sin, and take his victim to eternal bliss ! (*he rises*) now, I am yours !

Alm. Thou art heaven s ! offer one sacrifice and win its love for ever ! advance, advance ! (*he passes through the portal, hurrying Orasmyn after him*)

SCENE IV—*the apartment of Alraschid—the sleeping chamber—ottomans elevated form his couch, surmounted by a splendid canopy—an ante-chamber extends beyond, terminated by a portal—lights are burning in tripods, and two pages, apparently locked in slumber, lay near the entrance of the chamber—*CEPHANIA *enters cautiously through the portal, at the extremity of the scene.*

Ceph. I've gained the chamber—(*she advances*) how ! all in unguarded sleep !—Murteza ! Chebib ! slothful pages ! rouse. They stir not :—scarcely breathe ! some subtle, wicked charm lays all their faculties as in a death. Angels guard us ! (*she passes quickly onward to Alraschid's couch*) My lord ! my love ! my life !—Alraschid wake !—no word ?—what sorcery's here ?—no answer yet ? nay, triumph fiends ! and now fond heart despair. They come—the fatal pon-

G 2

ard gleams—mercy ! mercy ! heaven ! (*she conceals herself in the silken drapery which flows from the canopy beside the couch*)

ALMANZOR *and* ORASMYN *enter from the further portal, which closes after them—they advance till they stand opposite the couch of the caliph.*

Alm. Tis crowned !—o ! boundless joy ! our cause is crowned !—behold the tyrant bound in magic sleep ! god of my fathers ! thanks—eternal thanks ! all my triumphant wishes touch their verge—nay, my soul aches with transport. Strike, boy, strike !

Oras. One moment yet ; one little moment !

Alm. Tis heaven's command ; to pause would damn thee. Plunge the avenging poniard to his heart then on his dying ear shout terribly—" tis Ali's son who smites Alraschid !" (*he drags Orasmyn to the couch*) be sudden ! strike ! (*Orasmyn lifts his arm, Cephania suddenly casts herself forward to receive the blow*)

Ceph. Yea! strike ; with Ali's blood let Ali's poniard gleam !

Oras. (*drops the dagger and recoils*) Horror !— gods ! would I pierce a sister's bosom ?

Ceph. Murderer, strike !—a double sacrifice invites thy blow ; the wife will perish with her wedded lord.

Alm. Distracted wretch ! begone—avoid our fury !

Ceph. Never ! never ! here do I fix my everlasting hold. Avaunt ! detested homicides ! or my despairing cries shall call both men and gods to aid me.

Alm. Thy house's curse o'erwhelm thee, traitress ! thus let my rage——(*as he attempts to seize her, she snatches up the poniard Orasmyn has dropped at her feet, and repels him*)

Ceph. Ha ! my father's poniard arms my hand, and his great spirit nerves my heart. Hence, hoary ruffian, hence ! heaven and the tomb alike befriend my cause, and ghosts and angels combat by my side.

Alm. Perdition to my hopes ! thus, visionary wretch, to end thy dream ! (*he wrests the dagger from her hand, drags her forward, and is about to stab her*)

Oras. Hold! her blood is mine; spare my sister!

Alm. Then swift redeem her with a nobler victim.

Oras. (*refusing the dagger*) No, no, no! if the heavens claim a sacrifice, here let their thunder strike! I yield this wretched life a forfeit for my broken vows —but will not:—no, no, I cannot *murder!*

Ceph. Blessed be my brother! blessed! blessed!— (*she springs towards him, and they enfold each other*)

Alm. Perjured slave! may an eternal curse.— Rouse, maddening rage! inspire an old man's arm with dreadful force, and——

Oras. and Ceph. (*clinging to him*) Mercy! mercy!

Alm. Off, off! ye vile degenerate pair! the ancient lion rouses ere it dies, and thus devotes its latest prey! (*he breaks from them*)

Ceph. Yawn earth! and bury my despair! (*she dashes herself upon the ground—Orasmyn kneels by her side—Almanzor springs upon the couch to immolate his victim—at the moment his dagger is uplifted, the caliph starts from his apparent slumber, and catches the old man's arm—the curtains behind the couch spring aside, and archers, with their bows bent, form a wall around the prince—the hangings which cover the upper section of the front scene draw up, and exhibit an open saloon, extending over the architroon, brilliantly lighted, and filled with characters—at the front of its balustrade the various conspirators are ranged as captives, kneeling and surrounded by guards —the pages in the room beneath spring forward in attitudes, and the portal at the extremity of the scene opens, through which* GIAFAR *and attendants with torches enter—the entire grouping and illumination is instant and simultaneous*)

Alrasc. Thus heaven in thunder vindicates its own!

Alm. Cursed be the hour, cursed the false star that rules it, and damned the juggling tongue that tempted to betray!—is all o'erwhelmed! fiend! traitor! Æthiop! where art *thou?*

Alrasc. Behold him in thy sovereign and thy judge. Water hath cleansed the Æthiop's skin, but what blest unguent purifies a traitor's heart? (*he flies to Cephania and lifts her in his arms*) here let my wonder and my transport kneel! look up, excellent pattern of thy sex, and let a doting husband call thee back to life; nay, gaze upon the ring with which thou wert espoused. Ha! said I not truly, love? " Cephania is the Æthiop's bride."

Ceph. A strange confused intelligence dawns o'er me; I know not yet if it be joy or pain—yet sure *those* lips are harbingers of blessings only!

Alrasc. Forgive too hard a trial of thy glorious faith—that e'er I doubted is my lasting shame.

Giaf. (advancing with the arab) My prince! rather on your slave that shame should fall :—my jealous caution was the cause of each deceit. Lady! view well this arab's face.

Ceph. Ha! Almanzor's, my stern uncle's slave, who——

Arab Yea, that wretched man, whose fatal negligence betrayed a noble master's cause, and crushed the glorious hopes of all his tribe. Nay, I deserve thy curse.

Alrasc. Perchance her blessing, rather. A providence, disguised like chance, disclosed through this vile worm a mighty plot. Life and empire moved but half my care. But oh! Cephania's love! a doubt of that were madness. I knew not if her heart were truly mine. I dreaded lest her kinsmen's wiles—ah, love! forgive such thoughts ;—I wound about thee a close studious snare : thy women were counselled to my purpose, perpetual stratagem beset thy steps, whilst I, impenetrably shrouded, watched o'er all.

Ceph. Ha! it dawns more clear, and now the full conviction flashes to my heart. Oh! thou dear impostor, these gushing tears must chide thee, not my words. But oh! one boon, one dear, *dear* boon. (*she takes Orasmyn's hand, then looks pleadingly in Alraschid's face*) Orasmyn is Cephania's brother.

Alrasc. He is Alcæschid's! in this fraternal pressure we twine the olive round our father's graves. (*they em-*

brace) For his dear sake let mercy wildly cover an offending tribe.   Hear all of Ali's blood ! my vanquished enemies ! Orasmyn's friendship and Cephania's love are your accepted ransom.   Live ! be free, be happy ! thus doth Alraschid vindicate his reign. (*the various conspirators cast themselves in postures of homage —Almanzor alone remains erect*)

Alm. Apostates ! recreants without a name ! ay, kneel to man : be spurned by heaven ! bless your destroyer, and so curse yourselves ! still one unconquerable spirit soars beyond the reach of shame.   Yea, Alraschid ! usurper ! tyrant ! Almanzor, faithful to his godlike stock, still curses thee in bitterness of soul. Thus compassed round by hireling slaves, my honest lip still bids thee tremble.   Thy mercy ! mercy from thee ! ha ! ha ! dare not mock me, vain one, dare not ! mark me ! if e'er again this arm is free, again it grasps a poniard ! again it menaces a tyrant's heart.

Alrasc. (*after a pause*) Giafar, swear to me an oath : whatever fate betide thy prince, this man in safety passes from my court.   Swear !

Giaf. By allah and his prophet, yea !

Alrasc. (*advancing to Almanzor*) Almanzor, thou hast termed me TYRANT—am I that name ? search thy heart deeply, and inquire the truth.   If thou didst wrong me, let justice triumph over passion ; but if the accusation stand confirmed, thy foe and the world's enemy are one.   Satisfy thyself, and redress thy fellow-creatures. (*gives his dagger to Almanzor, and presents his breast to meet it*)

Alm. (*trembling with contending passions*) Thou *art* a tyrant—a very tyrant ! for thou wilt not leave thy foe even the liberty to hate. (*he drops the dagger*)

Alrasc. O glad return of wandered nobleness ! thus let my arms——

Alm. (*recoiling*) Nay, by your leave—we touch not ; I wish no more to hate, but feel I ne'er can love.   For fifteen years I lived but while I cursed thee.   Well, well ! 'tis o'er.   I'll to my desert ; live but a little to forget the world, and be myself forgotten ! (*as he turns to quit the scene, Orasmyn springs to him and clasps his knees)*

Oras. Uncle ! uncle ! you reared me, fostered me ; shall I forsake you now ? o, my full heart ! no, no. Lead to the desert, uncle ! I'll follow you till death !

Alm. My boy ! my sweetest nursling ! death hath no pang past quitting thee. Nay, by these tears—this kiss—tis so——*(suddenly he snatches Orasmyn to his heart, then places him between Alraschid and Cephania)* take him—he is yours ! farewell ! farewell !

                         [he rushes out

Oras. Nay, hear me uncle ! hear your faithful boy !

Ceph. *(restraining him)* Rest thee, beloved Orasmyn ! anon, our uncle's stormy passions will, with a natural cadence sink ; and peace, like a fine soft rainbow, meekly settle on his closing day. O ! ye dear rivals ! how am I blessed to blend you in my heart ! there live to reign for ever—there in holiest brotherhood divide your own ! *(she folds their hands in each others)*

FINALE.

Joy ! joy ! joy !
Raise the shout, and pierce the skies !
Love is born, as hatred dies,
    Arabian boy !
Allah crowns thy destinies,
    Joy ! joy ! joy !

THE END OF THE ÆTHIOP.

OVERTURE

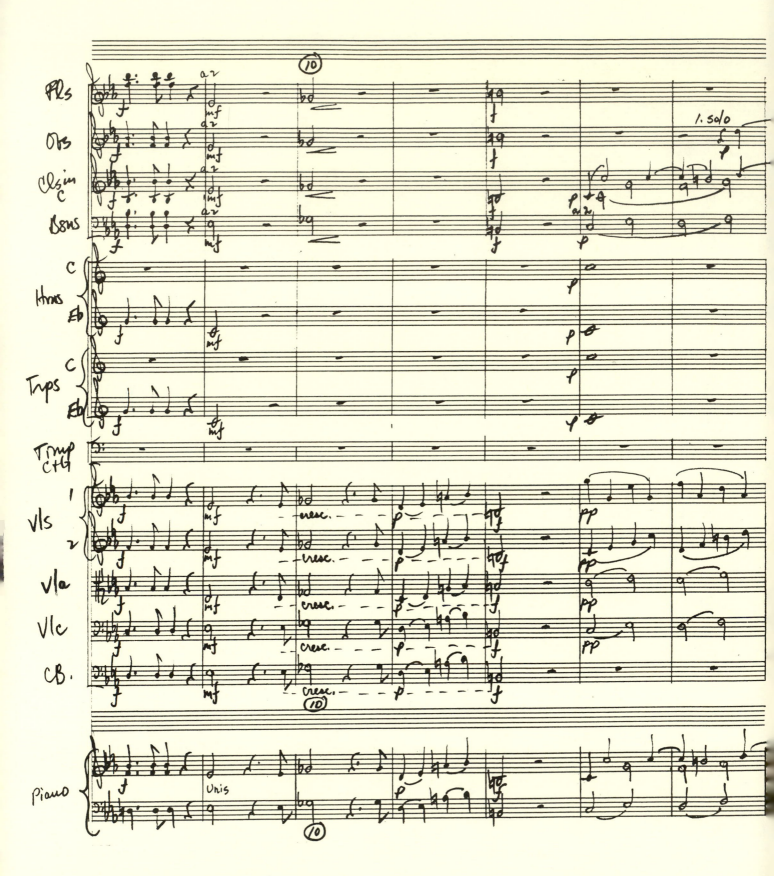

3

158

Allegretto

Larghetto

RONDO
Allegro

164

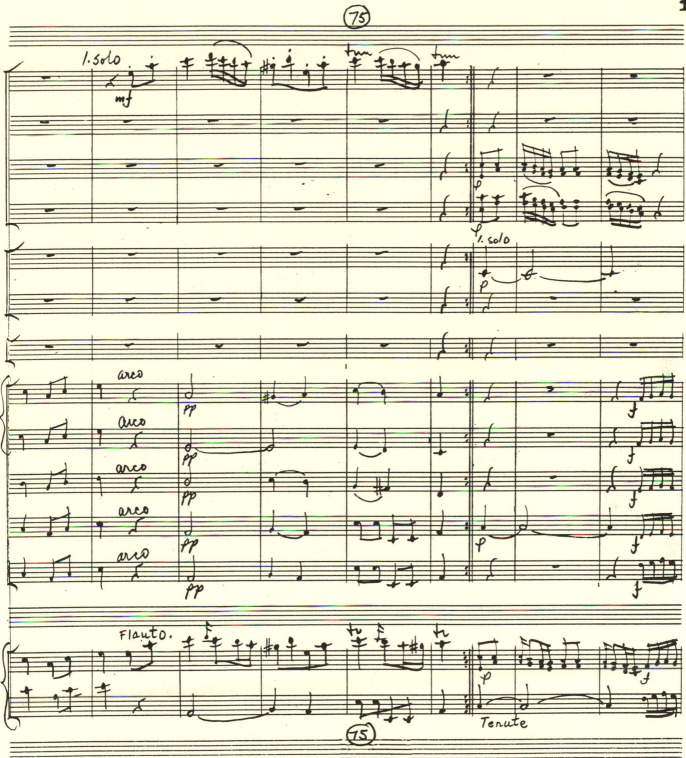

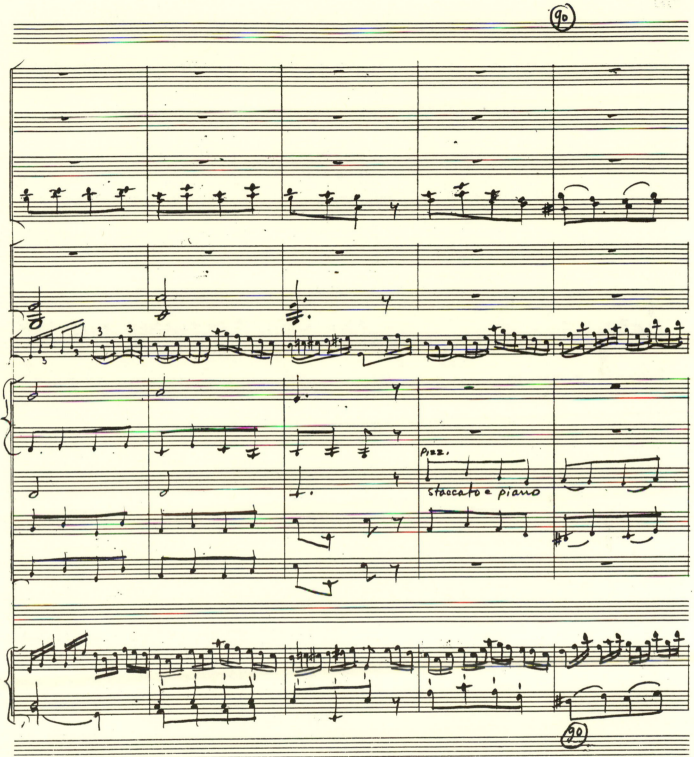

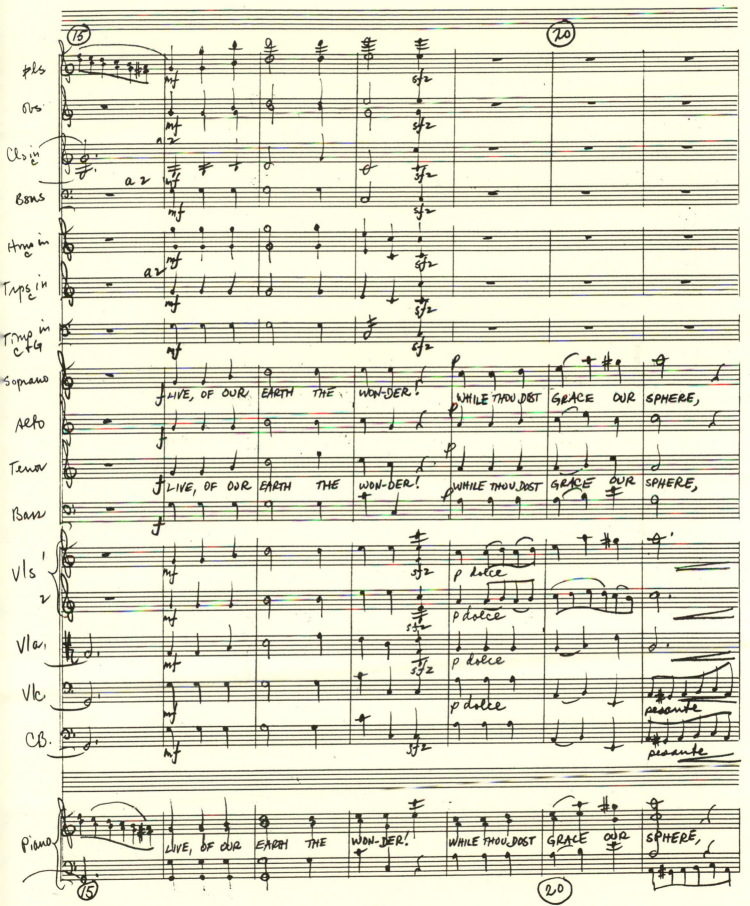

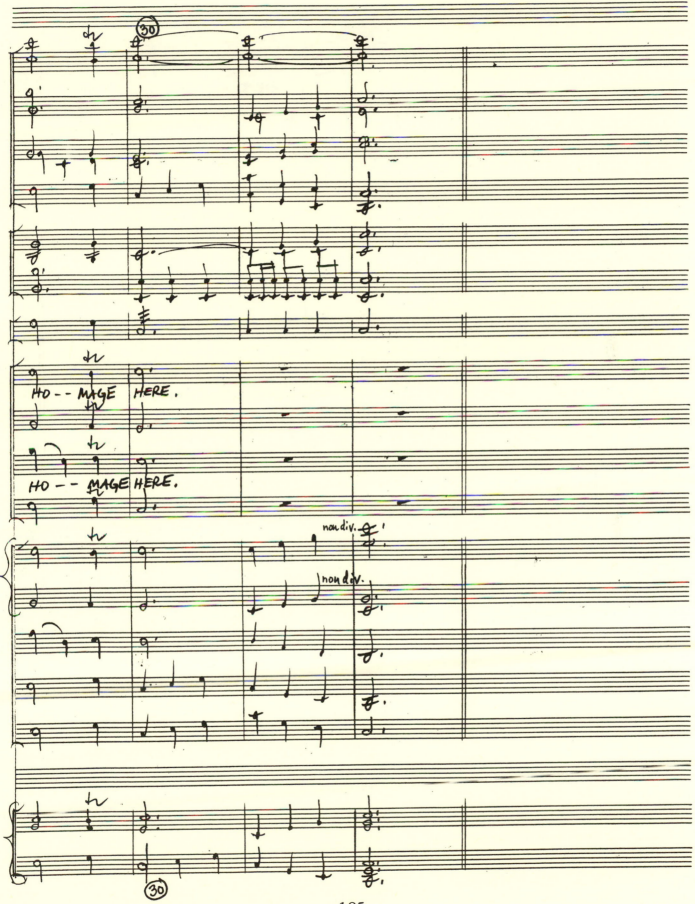

185

32

188

20
1 solo
p
a2
p
DING, DING, DONG I
HEARD IT PLAY, ME-
THOUGHT ITS JIN-GLE
SEEM'D TO SAY WITH
BURNING NOON WILL
COME THE TIME A-
ARCO
ARCO
DING, DING, DONG, I
HEARD IT PLAY, ME-
THOUGHT ITS JIN-GLE
SEEM'D TO SAY WITH
BURNING NOON WILL
COME THE TIME A-
20

34

190

Moderato.

A tempo
15
Fl.
Obs
Bsns
Horns in G
Zoe
Benmoussaff
Vls. 1 2
Vla
Vlc.
CB.
Piano
sfz p colla voce
A tempo
MIGHTY MAN! THOUGH RI-VALS LANGUISH, SWEAR YOUR LOVE SHALL NE-VER STRAY
I SWEAR! EVER! O, EVER!
Benmoussaff.
Zoe
I SWEAR! EVER! O. EVER! MIGHTY MAN! THOUGH RIVALS LANGUISH, SWEAR YOUR LOVE SHALL NEVER STRAY-
ad libitum
15

196

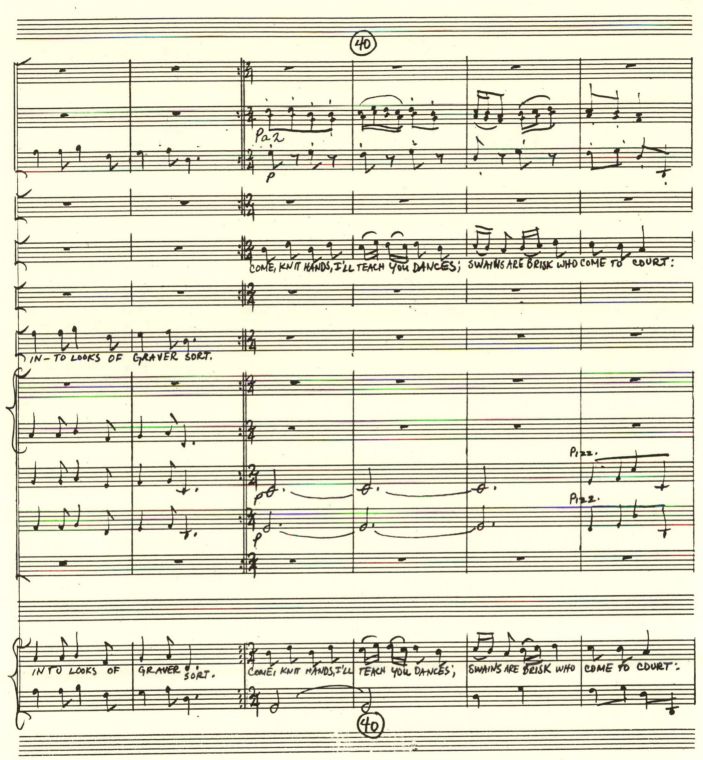

46

HOW SOON ARE THE HOURS
DUET

48

204

50

30
p dolce
TRUE, ON NO DAINTIES ARE FED, BUT LIGHT ARE OUR SPIRITS, AS LIGHTLY WE SUP AND THE
p dolce
BUT LIGHT ARE OUR SPIRITS, AS LIGHTLY WE SUP AND THE
con sord.
p dolce
con sord.
p dolce
con sord.
p dolce
con sord.
p dolce
Duetto.
Zoe
Alexis
TRUE, ON NO DAINTIES ARE FED, BUT LIGHT ARE OUR SPIRITS, AS LIGHTLY WE SUP AND THE
30

52

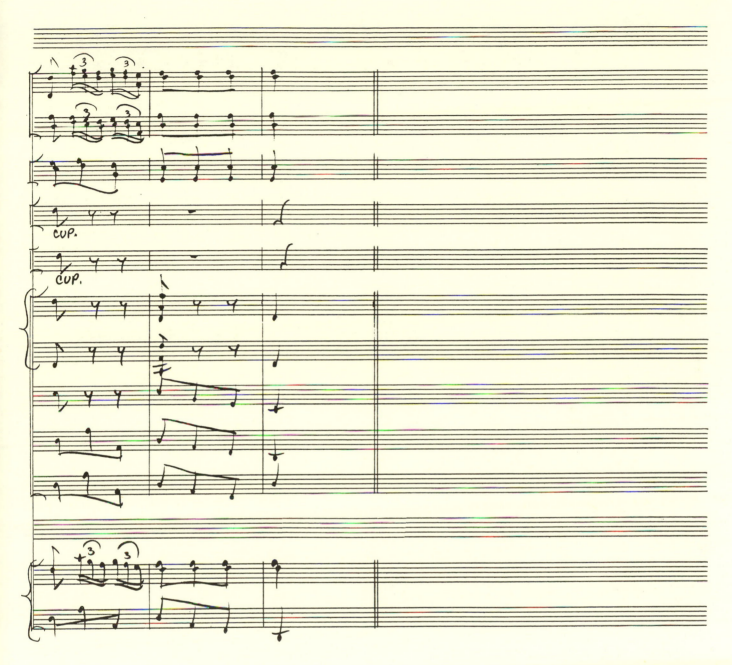

54

5
p
1 solo
MERCHANDIZE CRYING, WITH
CUSTOMERS BUYING, WITH
FOLK IN ALL STATIONS, WITH
GOODS FROM ALL NATIONS, WITH
MERCHANDIZE CRYING, WITH
CUSTOMERS BUYING, WITH
FOLK IN ALL STATIONS, WITH
GOODS FROM ALL NATIONS, WITH
PIZZ.
MERCHANDIZE CRYING, WITH
CUSTOMERS BUYING, WITH
FOLK IN ALL STATIONS, WITH
GOODS FROM ALL NATIONS, WITH
5

Allegro
a2
a2
a2
a2
a2
a2
O, THE BEZESTEIN IS MERRY MERRY MERRY, FOR O, THE BEZESTEIN IS MERRY MERRY MERRY.
O, THE BEZESTEIN IS MERRY MERRY MERRY, FOR O, THE BEZESTEIN IS MERRY MERRY MERRY.
O, THE BEZESTEIN IS MERRY MERRY MERRY, FOR O, THE BEZESTEIN IS MERRY MERRY MERRY.

220

DANCE IN THE ETHIOP.
Siciliano.

Andante grazioso

MUSICAL COLLOQUY.

A-WAY TO THE PRISON! GUARDS DRAG HIM AWAY

POWDER I PRAY!

FOR A CUDGEL TO POUND THEE TO

POWDER I PRAY!

OH, HEAR HOW HE SWEARS!

FURIES FIRE AND FURIES!

Guards A-WAY, A-WAY, CHORUS THE LAW IS RE-GARDLESS OF THREATS OR OF PRAY'RS, THE LAW IS RE-

Alexis: FIRE AND FURIES
Guards Ben: Cho: in 3 parts.
FURIES A-WAY, AWAY, Oh, HEAR HOW HE SWEARS! THE LAW IS RE-GARDLESS OF THREATS OR OF PRAY'RS, THE LAW IS RE-

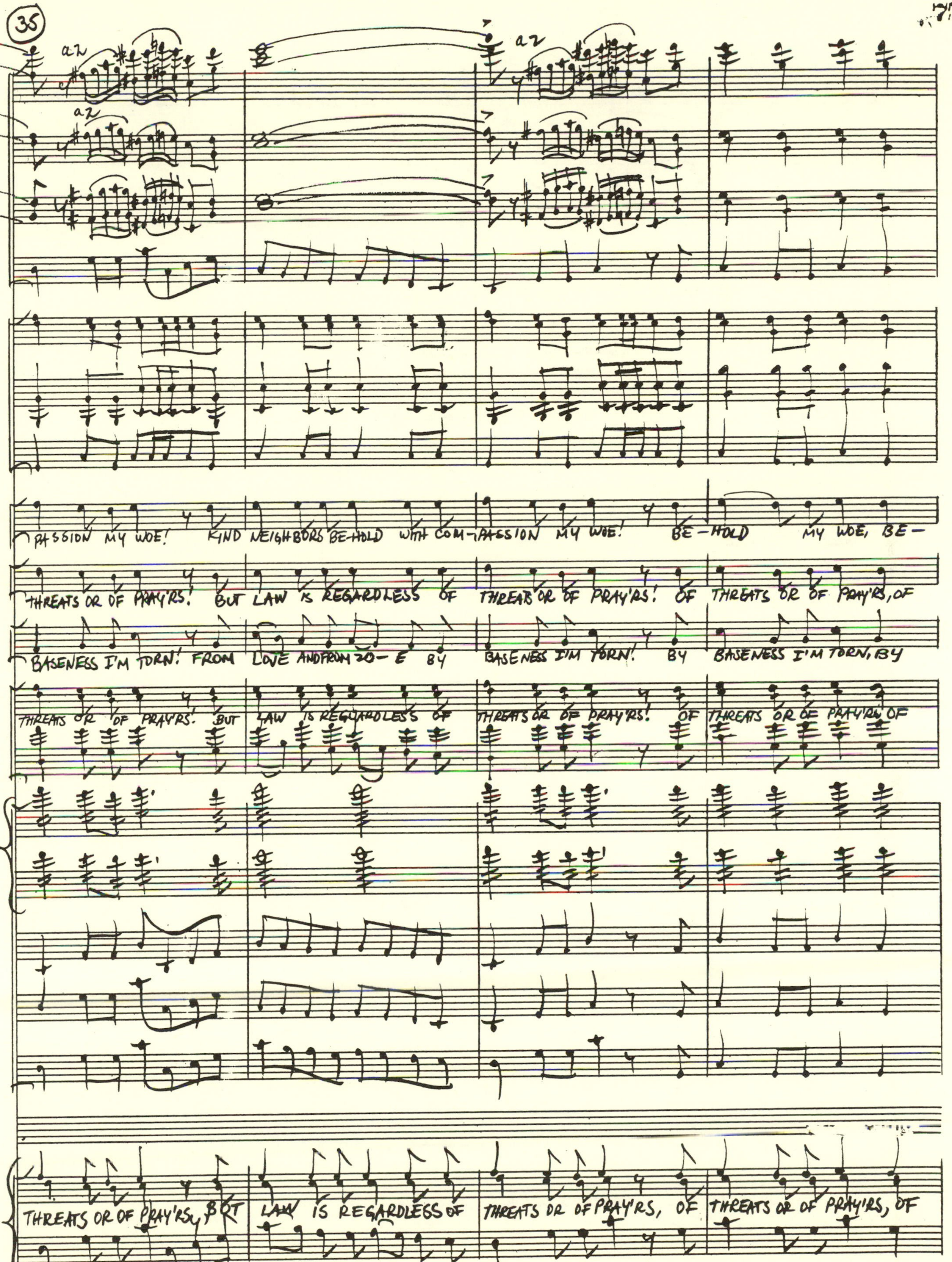

78
40
Fls
a2
Obs
Cls in C
Bsns
Hrns in C
Trps in C
Timp in C+G
Zoe
HOLD MY WOE!
Ben
THREATS OR OF PRAY'RS!
Alexis
BASENESS I'M TORN!
Guards + Chorus
THREATS OR OF PRAY'RS!
Vls 1 2
Vla
Vlc.
CB.
Piano
THREATS OR OF PRAY'RS!
40

235

80

236

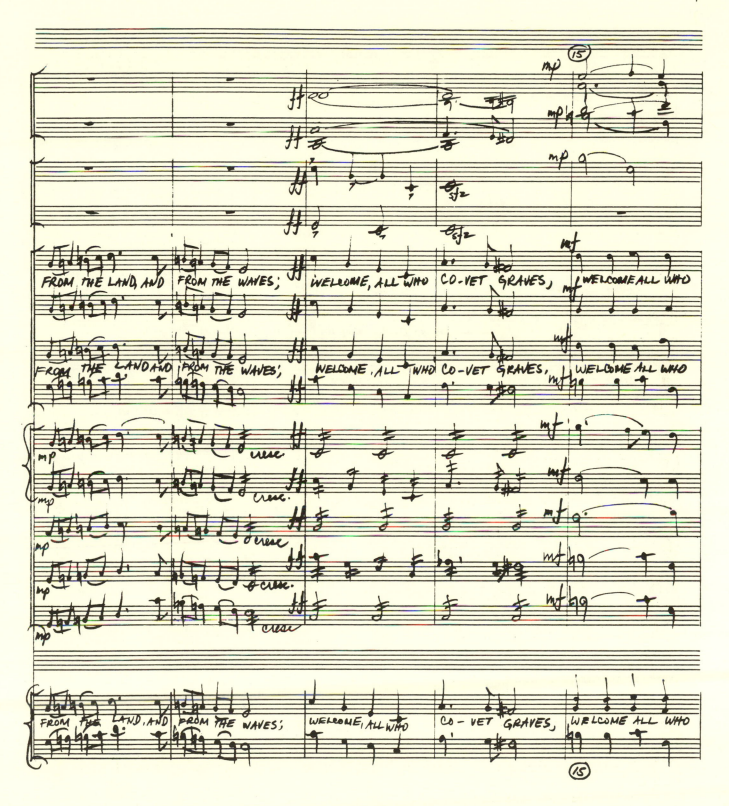

AS THE RED MOON THRO' VAP' - - - - - RISH SKIES! THRO' VAP' - - -

AS THE RED MOON THRO' VAP' - - - - - RISH SKIES! THRO' VAP' - - - -

AS THE RED MOON THRO' VAP' - - - - - RISH SKIES!

- - - AS THE RED MOON THRO' VAP' - - - - - - RISH SKIES! THRO' VAP'

86

242

88

244

NOURREDDIN, AT THE TOP OF THE CATACOMB.

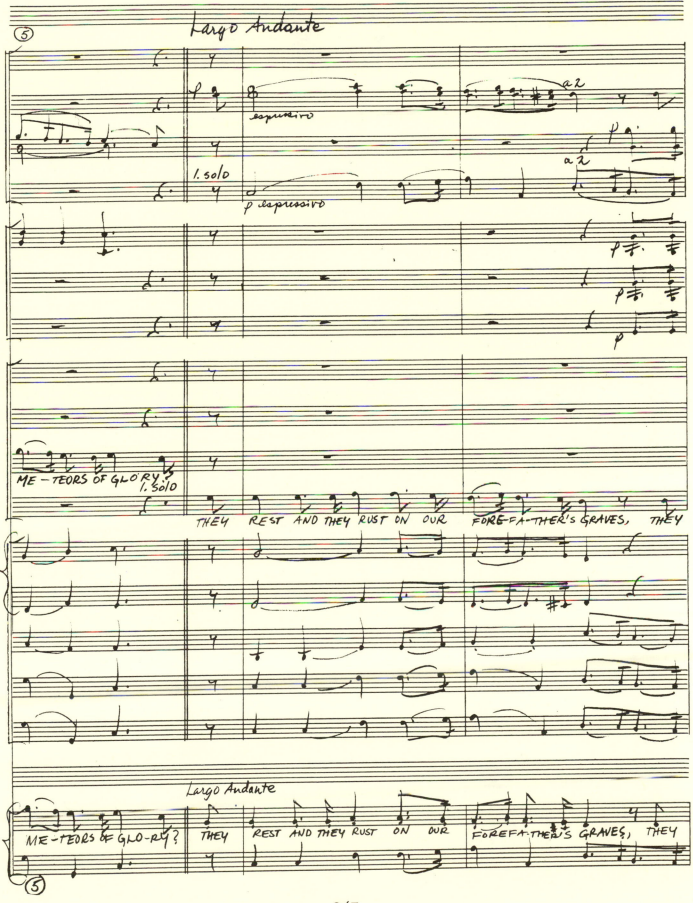

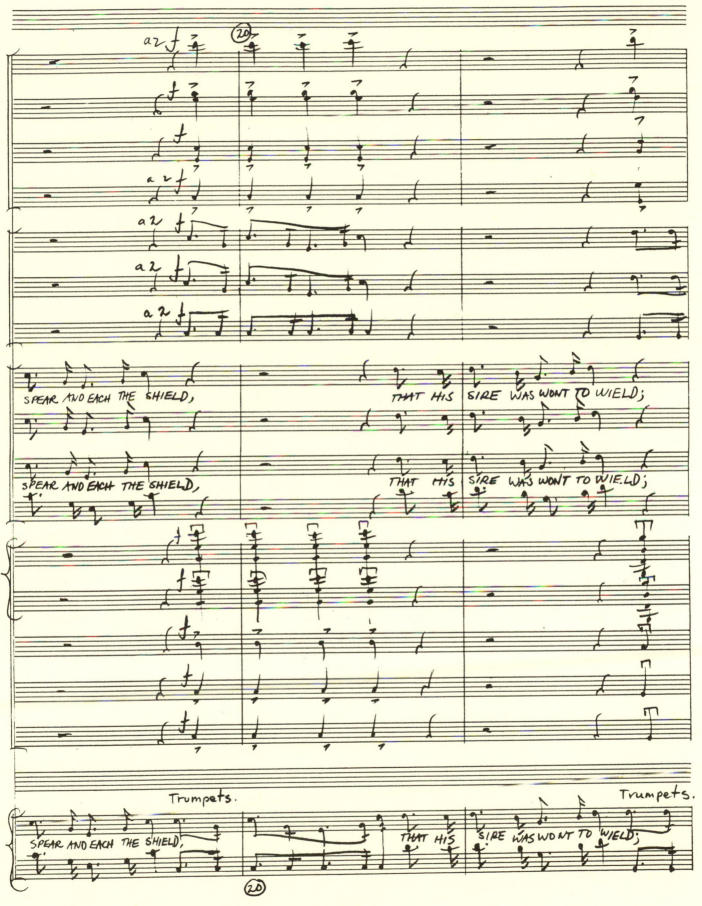

TY-RANTS! OF THE FRAY BE-WARE! TY-RANTS! OF THE FRAY BE-WARE!

TY-RANTS! OF THE FRAY BE-WARE! TY-RANTS! OF THE FRAY BE-WARE!

TYRANTS! OF THE FRAY BE-WARE! TYRANTS! OF THE FRAY BE-WARE!

98

254

WORD TO MY HUSBAND I FIRST FAIN WOULD SAY, FAL LAL DE RAL, LA RA FAL, LAL DE RA LA, FAL

WORD TO MY HUSBAND I FIRST FAIN WOULD SAY, FAL LAL DE RAL, LA RA FAL, LAL DE RA LAL, FAL

113

268

FINALE.

ALLAH CROWNS THY DESTINIES. ALLAH CROWNS THY DESTINIES.

ALLAH CROWNS THY DESTINIES. ALLAH CROWNS THY DESTINIES.

ALLAH CROWNS THY DESTINIES. ALLAH CROWNS THY DESTINIES.

CONTENTS OF THE SERIES